CHASING

the

Dragon

*A Former Narcotics Detective's Journey
Through Drug Addiction, Prison,
And Recovery*

CHASING

the

Dragon

A Former Narcotics Detective's Journey
Through Drug Addiction, Prison,
And Recovery

HAL NEVITT

Jones Media Publishing
10645 N. Tatum Blvd. Ste. 200-166
Phoenix, AZ 85028
www.JonesMediaPublishing.com

Disclaimer:

The author strives to be as accurate and complete as possible in the creation of this book, notwithstanding the fact that the author does not warrant or represent at any time that the contents within are accurate due to the rapidly changing nature of the Internet. Some of the names and locations of stories told may have been changed for privacy.

While all attempts have been made to verify information provided in this publication, the Author and the Publisher assume no responsibility and are not liable for errors, omissions, or contrary interpretation of the subject matter herein. The Author and Publisher hereby disclaim any liability, loss or damage incurred as a result of the application and utilization, whether directly or indirectly, of any information, suggestion, advice, or procedure in this book. Any perceived slights of specific persons, peoples, or organizations are unintentional.

Printed in the United States of America

ISBN: 978-1-948382-51-9 paperback

TABLE OF CONTENTS

INTRODUCTION

*T*his is the true life story of a former police officer and undercover narcotics detective who while hunting cocaine dealers became addicted to the very substance that he was seeking to rid from the streets.

Follow along into the darkness of addiction, the brutal reality of imprisonment, and the eventual release and redemption of one man who has seen the dragon, chased the dragon, been caught and mauled by the dragon, and, through Grace, has lived to tell about it.

My story isn't easy to tell, because I am not proud of everything I have done. But it is what it is, and as I recount my journey, I promise to pull no punches, to tell you why I made the decisions I made (as uncomfortable as it is), and to convincingly prove that, if a guy like me can be pulled off the scrap heap and used by God to spread His message of hope, then He can do the same for you--NO ONE is beyond redemption.

As I look back over my life and the ugliness I allowed to become part of it, I am filled with gratitude that the God of all creation would bestow justice, mercy, and grace upon me. It seems nearly incomprehensible that a man who set out with the honorable intention of taking drugs off the street became addicted, then arrested, convicted, and imprisoned, but now has been forgiven, redeemed, and saved by the grace of God!

I am especially grateful to my wife, Ellen Nevitt, for her non-judgmental way of dealing with me; to my children Kevin, Collin, and Mariah (AKA Mighty Mo) for their love, and constant energy;

and to my mother, Mickie Nevitt, for her endless encouragement, faithfulness, and love.

I cannot possibly name all those who positively impacted me but here are a few: Bill and Ann Stuart, Paul and Pat Johnson, Gene Richards, Kevin Chadwick, Mark Gleason, Ray Klies, Paul Arnold, Eric Dermer, Tony Legault, Carter Crile, Mark Barnett, Mike Hannifan, Steve Little, Scott Rhodes, Nancy Greenlee, Bob VanWyck, Chis McBride, Joe and Rae Chornenky, Tom Higgins, Rafael Gallego, Frank Saverino, Rick and Tana Canfield, Kevin Reugg, Mike Sucher, and Tracy Ward. Everyone from Oasis Community Church!

A special Thank You to Pete Wooster who helped in so many ways particularly with encouraging me to write even when it hurt.

Here is my story.

Chapter 1

CHILDHOOD OF CONFLICT

Convicted felon, cocaine addict, alcoholic, crooked cop: sounds like a movie plotline rather than how I would have envisioned describing myself. But the truth of the matter is I have been that guy.

A question I often ask myself is how a "normal" kid with a "normal" upbringing veers so far off track. I suppose the key thought in that statement is "normal," and how one defines it. I felt like I grew up in a typical home in Scottsdale, Arizona, with maybe a few deviations along the way. My mother divorced my biological father when I was very young; met and married Howard Nevitt in Kodiak, Alaska; and moved us to the Phoenix area in 1964. My stepfather adopted my sister and me in 1966, and while we weren't the "well off" part of society, we lived well enough. Both of my parents were hard workers with blue collar occupations.

My mom worked three jobs: she was a waitress, a bookkeeper, and a personal assistant to a number of older adults, who came to completely depend on her for their assorted needs. She would do everything from shuttling them to and from doctors' appointments, to taking them grocery shopping, to managing their finances. She was also a devoted homemaker, and the glue that held our family together. Her gift of hospitality was renowned among our friends and extended family: she went all out when people came over for dinner by making sure she had everyone's favorite dish prepared, no matter how many she had to cook. Mom worked non-stop both inside and outside the home until the day she was admitted to the hospital shortly before her death. She finally succumbed to a third recurrence of cancer at age 78.

My dad was a bartender for most of his life, working long hours at several places around town; eventually, he saved enough money to buy his own tavern. The week he took ownership, I helped clean the floor mats and ready the place to reopen under new management, and I remember how proud I was of him and his accomplishments. Over the years, I spent many hours at the tavern, getting to know some of the regulars, playing pinball, watching people drink, and hanging out with my dad. So, in a way, drinking and alcohol really were just a normal part of growing up for me.

At age 12, I took my first drink. And it wasn't just a sip from my mother's glass of wine or my dad's beer-- it was full-on intoxication. By that age, I had already watched a number of my relatives getting drunk regularly, so it seemed like a natural progression for me to follow down the same path. My father drank daily, as did his father. And my grandmother, who downed whiskey shots, unintentionally taught me how to hide how much I had been drinking. Her favorite method was to pour Canadian Club into a glass of water, and because the whiskey separated from the water at the top, she could drink off the whiskey and ask for a refill with no one the wiser!

Consuming alcohol was a customary practice when my relatives got together, whether it was a special occasion or not. Often, the result was loud, obnoxious, and inadvertently entertaining behavior, such as adults clumsily falling out of chairs or the incidental expulsion of bodily fluids, which usually ended up on my mom's couch or the hallway carpet. Though my mom clearly didn't approve of my father's drinking and made her objection known continually throughout the years, he wouldn't or couldn't stop for any sustained period of time. His lack of restraint usually led to my mom taking drastic measures.

On a fairly regular basis, my mom packed up us kids and took us somewhere to stay away from home until things settled down.

Of course, my sister and I thought it was quite the adventure. One time, we stayed at the Kon Tiki Motel in Phoenix, an impressively large motel that, to me, seemed like a fancy place where rich people stayed. The massive Tiki torches all around the grounds, at the entrance, and flickering on the water in the pool are forever etched in my memory. It was a special place, although I remember feeling a little sad that we were all together in this "nice hotel" while my dad was all alone. Upon returning home from our "getaways," dad would be more attentive and everything would be all right for a while, but, inevitably, the pattern would be repeated. I think that at some point, after my sister and I were grown and had left the house, my mom simply acquiesced: nothing she did ever made my dad change his behavior.

Another adventure relating to the role alcohol played in my "normal" childhood took place when my dad's oldest brother came from Illinois to visit. He was also a heavy drinker, and he and my dad always seemed to have a jovial time together drinking throughout the day. This particular incident transpired when my dad and uncle went to a topless bar on Van Buren Street (at that time a very seedy area of downtown Phoenix) to conduct business, and decided to let me tag along. I suppose since they knew their purpose in going there wasn't for the show, they had no compunction about bringing along a 10-year old. When we arrived in the middle of the day, I was directed to sit down in a booth in a dark corner. Even as a young boy, I could appreciate the scantily clad ladies who provided me with popcorn and soda as they tousled my hair (yes, I had hair then) and made a fuss over me. At that point, I was feeling very mature, having come to a place where men hung out and beautiful women paid attention to me.

In actuality, my dad and uncle were there to confront one of the patrons regarding the repayment of money he owed them. From what I could surmise, my uncle's primary function was to educate this individual about the relationship between prompt payment and maintenance of his current health status. After several minutes of heated conversation, raised voices and swearing, my dad and uncle maneuvered the guy through a back door that led into an alley. I could hear heavy thuds from the outside wall, and I sat there anxiously hoping that it wasn't my family that was in trouble. A little while later, my dad and uncle came back unscathed, followed shortly by the patron who looked pretty roughed up and immediately headed to the restroom. In retrospect, I readily admit that this was an inappropriate scene for a child to witness, but at the time, I thought it was pretty cool that my dad and uncle were real live tough guys.

My mother must have had an intuition about some of the questionable behavior I was exposed to and was concerned how it would influence me, because a couple of years later, my parents unexpectedly decided that my sister and I should attend church, even though they did not. The problem was that church was on Sunday, and as an avid football fan, I already had standing plans for my Sundays. I was pretty resentful that I had to go and sit through a church service, while my dad got to stay home and watch the games. Consequently, my irritation inhibited any chance of learning much about God or the Bible. So, the summer after eighth grade, when I was fourteen, my folks came up with an even more ingenious plan: "Send Hal to summer camp!"

Grudgingly, I agreed to go, and fortunately for me, it was not what I expected. Prescott Pines was in a beautiful, mountainous setting about an hour and a half north of Phoenix, and for a boy who loved the outdoors and outdoor activities like softball and hiking, it was a wonderful place to ditch the summer heat. I found myself enjoying the change of pace and settling into a comfortable routine. Of course, the purpose of the camp, aside from having fun, was to learn about God and His Son, Jesus Christ. And learn I did! I learned about the sacrifice Jesus made when He gave up His life on the cross, and how by God raising Him from the dead, I had been given the gift of eternal life. I even stood up during one of our evening sessions and professed my acceptance of Jesus Christ as my Lord and Savior. It was a significant moment in my life. I am so grateful that my parents insisted that I go to that camp, even though they may not have realized the full impact it would have on my life.

There are many things I am thankful for concerning my parents and the way they brought me up. I know they did their best, and instilled in me values that I have in turn tried to instill in my own children. These two industrious people taught me the benefits of hard work, perseverance, setting goals, and achievement. My work ethic, firm initiative, and attitude of "doing whatever it takes" are directly attributable to my parents' example. My parents also ingrained in me a deep-seated love for and loyalty to my country, which was instrumental in my selection of a future career.

But I also recognize that I am a product of both positive and negative influences experienced during my youth and adolescence. My relationship with alcohol and subsequent dependence upon it were outward manifestations of the negative. As I mentioned, I took my first drink of alcohol when I was 12 years old. My best friend and I pooled our allowance and commissioned his older sister to buy us a bottle of Spanada wine. Now Spanada could not be found on anyone's wine list; this stuff went for $2.50 for a half-gallon. We drank that whole bottle, and when my friend's sister returned with her date, we drank shots from the bottle of Old Granddad bourbon they had. And to top it off, we smoked a joint.

I recall how cool I thought it was to act like I was all grown up. Getting drunk was a way of life for a number of my relatives, so for me to follow down this path seemed like it was a normal part of growing up.

After all of that stuff, that is the wine, whiskey, and pot went off, an inch or so behind my belly button, I had my first memorable spiritual experience. I threw up. Both my friend and I experienced this at the same time. I can recall being out in the backyard of his home puking and I clearly recall me saying, "I'll never do this again." I didn't do the same thing again...for at least a week or so. Then it was right back at it. Now I didn't mix so much, but I was a regular weekend warrior with alcohol. All the way through high school I was drunk nearly every weekend.

My upbringing, whether one considers it normal or not, is not an excuse for the poor choices I made later in life. I am accountable for both the good and the bad consequences of my behavior, and it would only serve to delay amending my wrongs if I tried to project blame on anyone or anything else.

Chapter 2

SEMPER FI: AN INSTANT BOND

By age 17, the excitement and enthusiasm I felt when I accepted Christ had worn off, and I was focused on graduating from high school and figuring out what I would do next. So, toward the end of my senior year, a friend and I decided to join the Army on what used to be called the Buddy Plan: we spoke to the recruiter together and began the testing process, where we were subjected to a battery of physical and mental challenges. Being young, healthy, and in great shape, I breezed through all the tests with no problems. That is, until the final one. It was an exercise in which a technician held up a card with a collection of colored dots on it. The dots formed a circle and within the circle, there was allegedly a number that I was to identify. As he held up the first card, I couldn't see a number, so he tried again with a second card, and yet again, I saw no number. Third card: no number. We then deduced that I was, in fact, color blind, and this one seemingly minor issue was enough to disqualify me from joining the Army. I was devastated!

As I stood outside the office waiting for my friend to complete the signup process, feeling more than a little embarrassed that a middle linebacker on the varsity football team had been sidelined by a series of colored dots, a Marine Corps Recruiter Staff Sergeant walked by. Noticing my dejection, he asked, "Who pissed in your Cheerios?" Now, with his uniform blouse, trousers with razor sharp creases, and polished shoes, this man stood about 6'4" and exuded confidence and authority. I laughed nervously and told him that I had just been rejected by the Army. His voice boomed, "Outstanding! Praise God! Now tell me, son, why won't they let you join the Army?" I had barely uttered the words "color blind" when he responded with, "You are not color blind!" His absolute certainty made me stand up a little straighter. He then ordered me to follow him and said that he would prove once and for all that I was not color blind, and that it would be my good fortune to join an elite fighting organization known as the United States Marine Corps. Unbeknownst to him, I had wanted to be a Marine from the time I was very young because my sister's boyfriend was a Marine, and he would let me wear his service cover whenever he came to visit her. So, without hesitation, I followed the Staff Sergeant as he led me to the sidewalk near a busy intersection.

"We're going to do an experiment, Marine, and I want you to pay close attention," he commanded, as he placed his hands on my shoulders and squared me to the overhead traffic light. Pointing to the signal, he said, "Ok, what color is that red light?" I nearly fell over.

"I'm waiting, Marine! What color is that red light?"

"Well, sir, it's red."

"Outstanding! See, you are not color blind! But just to be sure, let's try one more. What color is that green light?"

"Green," was my instantaneous reply.

"See there, lad, I told you that you were not color blind. Now, let's go get you signed up!"

So off we went to his office, where I filled out the paperwork and enlisted. But it wasn't completely official; because I was only 17, I needed my parents' signatures. But before we arrived at my house, we took a little detour to Tom's Tavern, had a couple of beers (yes, I was a minor, but it didn't seem to matter), and the Staff Sergeant regaled me with stories and told me about his love for the Corps and our country. As I listened to him with rapt attention, I thought of my own regard for being an American, how I tear up when "The Star Spangled Banner" is sung and how angry I get when people do not stand up during the National Anthem, and I realized I had just met a kindred spirit. The significance of the choice I had just made nearly overwhelmed me and my heart swelled with patriotism. Even at that young age, I understood what a great honor it was to defend and serve my country.

Fortunately, my parents didn't take much convincing to agree. While my mother was reluctant, my father was ecstatic, but they both enjoyed the story of me first being color blind and then not being color blind. They were proud of me when I graduated from boot camp on my 18th birthday, and excited that I had the opportunity to follow my dreams.

My time in the Marine Corps taught me several important things that have stuck with me throughout my life, even during the darkest times. First, there is a bond of brotherhood that is shared by all the people who serve this great nation in the Armed Forces. The relationships I forged in the Corps defy time and space, in that "once a Marine, always a Marine," and, to this day, I remain in contact with many of my fellow Marines who are now scattered across the country. A fairly recent example of this lifelong brotherhood was in 2007, when I accompanied my son, Collin, on his eighth grade field trip to Washington, D.C. While there, I took him to the Marine Corps Barracks that houses the Silent Drill Team and the Marine Corps Band, hoping to tour the installation. But upon arrival at the Main Gate, we were informed by a very formal young lance corporal that they were not set up for tours. As we turned away somewhat disappointed, an impeccably dressed sergeant in his mid to late twenties bounded toward us, calling for us to wait. With an iron grip, he shook my hand and said, "I understand you are a former Marine: Semper Fi, and thank you for your service!" I replied, "Semper Fi and thank **you** for your service," and that was all it took for there to be an instant bond.

Second, freedom is precious and worth fighting for. I saw and experienced things in some of the countries I visited during my service that do not cease to remind me of how valuable freedom is, especially when you don't have it. From my incarceration, I know first-hand what it feels like to lose one's freedom and then, fortunately, gain it back. Never will I take it for granted!

Third, the values of honor, courage, commitment, decisiveness, dependability, tact, honesty, and unselfishness that I learned in the Marine Corps are not just character traits to admire. They are embedded so deeply in my psyche that even though they were compromised during my addiction to alcohol and cocaine, they now make up the man I have become in recovery. One of the Marine mantras is, "Never give up, never give in, and never willingly accept second best." I owe my relentless dedication to excellence to the Corps.

The foundation that the Marine Corps developed in me as a young man set the stage for my future. But in addition to the wonderful values it taught me, it was also a time of testing my boundaries and letting loose. It was a culture of young warriors, who thought themselves "bullet proof" because of their youth and vigor, and it didn't take much of an occasion for us to celebrate our accomplishments with weekend binges. Personally, my consumption of alcohol increased dramatically.

I had my first inkling that I might have an alcohol problem when I was home on leave from the Marine Corps, in December 1974. I had received orders to Okinawa, Japan, and was granted nearly a month of leave time prior to shipping out. My family had a long established tradition of meeting at my parents' home on Christmas Eve to have a nice dinner and open presents. I spent the day shopping for gifts and once finished with that I spent the afternoon drinking eggnog at a bar. Now I drank that special kind of eggnog with the rum/brandy in it. I got really drunk and drove home in a car that I had borrowed from my parents. I recall parking the car in the middle of the street, staggering inside the door with all the presents, dropping them on the living room floor and then ping-ponging off the walls of the hallway down to my bedroom where I finally passed out. I awoke the next morning full of guilt, shame, and remorse for this was the first time anyone in my family had seen me in this state. Now they knew who and what I really was. I mumbled some sort of half-hearted apology to my mom. I know she had been terribly disappointed at my behavior the night before, and I think that she was afraid of where this might take me.

I spent the rest of my leave time sober, but miserable. I also made sure that everyone around me knew that I was sober, and miserable. I tried my best to make others miserable too. I was really self-absorbed, and basically a jerk.

While in the Marine Corps, my alcohol use flourished. Some of that was expected. Kind of a cultural issue that had evolved over the years, although now there is a movement among governmental institutions to increase awareness of the negative aspects of alcohol use/abuse.

Chapter 3

RIDE ALONG

pon my discharge from the Marines in 1977, I returned home and enrolled at Scottsdale Community College, majoring in Business Administration. Things were going pretty well for me at 21 years of age: I had the privilege of playing on the school's championship football team and I continued to drink regularly, without thought as to how it could or would affect my future. I had not realized how much alcohol had permeated every facet of my life, until I went to class drunk one day and had to excuse myself to go throw up. This should have been a wake-up call, but I dismissed the idea that I should give up drinking and decided that I simply needed to control it better.

It was during this time that I got a call from an old high school friend, Roy, who had become an officer with the Tempe Police Department. He phoned to invite me to go on a "Ride-Along," in which a person spends an entire shift with an officer and his squad to see how typical activities are handled, such as traffic stops, accidents, domestic disputes, burglaries, and the like. The Ride-Along is a community outreach, as well as a way to provide potential recruits with "Show and Tell." The idea piqued my interest, so we set it up for a Friday night.

That Friday I headed to the station with eager anticipation. As I pulled into the parking area, an impressive Mounted Officer and his horse walked by, and I was immediately awestruck by his aura of authority. Before I entered the building to report for my tour, we chatted for a few moments and I found myself wondering if these were the kind of men I was going to see in action tonight? My excitement was palpable!

Before embarking on the evening's adventure, I had to fill out the requisite paperwork, consisting of my name, date of birth, a waiver of liability, and other personal data for their records. Basically, they were asking me to sign on the dotted line that if they did something to hurt or kill me, I wouldn't hold them responsible. And I found out later that they also ran a criminal background check, as well as a wants/warrants check on me while I was in the waiting room. Finally, it was time for me to proceed into the Squad Room with Roy.

The door that led into the squad room had reached epic proportions in my mind: it was the divider between the general public and the select few who had become police officers, who had the respect of the community, varying levels of power, and defined common goals by which they all operated. The atmosphere of camaraderie was akin to what I felt in the Marines, so when Roy's squad mates good naturedly bantered with me, I felt right at home. They gave me condolences about having to ride with Roy, asking if they could have my truck, since it was a given that I would not survive the night in his care. A few noticed my military bearing, while others noted my good physical condition from playing football, and it was suggested that I might want to think about becoming a police officer. Now, when the people who know what it takes and have been through the entire process made that kind of suggestion, I knew I should give it due consideration. Could I be one of them?

The shift began in the briefing room, where we sat in classroom style chairs that faced the front. When the Sergeant entered, talking ceased. Without saying a word, this man commanded the respect and attention of everyone in the room as he made his way to the podium to address the group. He then briefed the squad on the events that occurred during the previous shift and recent trends in community criminal activity, and he sought input from the group on how to more effectively patrol the area and catch bad guys. Near the end of this give-and-take, he made note that Roy had a "rider," and that we were to see him at the conclusion. He wanted to make sure that I understood I was to observe only, not participate, as well as follow orders from Roy without question. I acknowledged this direction and we left the room to start our tour.

Throughout the shift, I watched in fascination as these men responded to calls for service, including family fights, drunks creating disturbances, and a robbery in progress. They made traffic stops, investigated accidents, and wrote reports on what they heard, observed, and did, and by the end of the night, I was thoroughly impressed with how they handled dangerous, emotionally charged events with calm, measured verbal tones and professionalism. I didn't want to leave. As I drove home afterwards, my mind was reeling with the possibility of becoming a policeman.

All weekend I thought about my experience. One of the things that was most attractive to me, a young man wanting to distinguish himself from the crowd and make his mark on society, was that people did what they were told to do by these men, and everywhere we went, people took notice of their presence. Admittedly, the sense of power and of being able to tell other people what to do greatly appealed to me. But it was more than that: watching how these men interacted with each other and the public, and how the public perceived and responded to them drew me in. There was also a brotherhood, much like I had experienced in the Marines and sorely missed since I'd been out, that called to me. By the time Monday morning rolled around, my decision was made. Focused on my mission, I went to Scottsdale Community College, changed my major to Administration of Justice, and then proceeded to hound Roy several times a week for "insider" information about the force.

When I graduated in the summer of 1978 with my Associate's Degree, I heard that the City of Scottsdale was hiring police assistants, who were charged with paperwork details, accident investigation, and other tasks while in training to become police officers. After submitting a job interest card, I was contacted by the Personnel

Department and invited to participate in a four-phase eligibility process: a written exam, a physical fitness test, an oral interview, and a polygraph. It was at the interview that I first officially met Sergeant Dale Samuels, Major Mike Gannon, and Captain Roy Finch.

I had already met Sergeant Samuels informally. About a month prior to the interview, while riding my motorcycle one night, a vehicle pulled out in front of me and, to avoid a collision, I had to crash the bike into the pavement. Stunned, I laid there a few minutes assessing my injuries. When I was finally able to get up and move myself and my bike off the road, a Scottsdale police officer came along. With a couple of broken ribs and a serious case of road rash, I clearly needed medical attention, so the officer called for an ambulance. But I had no money or insurance, and the thought of how much the ambulance was going to cost scared me more than the accident. I informed him that I would rather ride my motorcycle home. Well, he was not taking "no" for an answer, and called his supervisor to the scene, to whom I had to explain again that I just wanted to go home. Reluctantly, they consented, and the sergeant instructed the officer to follow me home, which he did.

That sergeant, who had responded to the scene of my wreck, was the same Sergeant Samuels who now sat on my oral board interview panel. He told the others, all of whom would eventually become my supervisors, that he was impressed with my ability to drive a motorcycle with the extent of my injuries. They asked if I had learned anything from that experience. I can't remember exactly what I said, but it had something to do with errant drivers, and it must have been the right answer because they all had a good laugh.

The final step of the process was the polygraph, which I found to be the most nerve-racking. The man who administered the test was very nice and tried to put me at ease by asking routine questions before progressing to more pointed questions about honesty, drug use, sex stuff, and so forth. After what seemed like eight hours, but in reality, was only one, he told me that I passed and it wouldn't be long before I was hired. The next chapter of my life was about to begin and I couldn't wait!

Chapter 4

LET'S BECOME
A POLICE OFFICER

While I was still in school at SCC, I met a lovely young woman named Karen Hayes in one of my administration of justice classes, and we began dating. She actually graduated ahead of me and went on a backpacking trip through Europe on her way to visit her parents, who were working in Iran. By the time she returned to Arizona in 1978, I had earned my Associate's Degree and had been hired as a police assistant with the Scottsdale Police Department. This was an unarmed civilian position designed to perform mundane activities, like taking report calls, directing traffic, and writing parking tickets, so that police officers would be freed up to enforce laws, make arrests, and respond to emergency situations. To others, this might have seemed like nothing extraordinary, but to me, it was the fulfillment of a dream. My foot was in the door!

My first assignment was on the day shift of Team 3, riding with Field Training Officer (FTO) Dennis Borkehhagen. He was an experienced veteran, whom I admired and respected, and he had no problem letting me cut my teeth on various types of reports. One incident stands out during my initial training with him: we were called to a domestic dispute involving two gay men and their dog, and I had to wait outside the home because this type of call was considered too volatile for an unarmed civilian. One of the men had decided to leave the relationship, and at issue was who would get custody of their small terrier, Muffin. As the participants emerged from the house, I observed how the heavily armed, officers successfully mediated the disagreement between the two men about "Muffin!" It was quite a sight!

Approximately a month later, I was transferred from the day shift to the swing shift (3:00 pm – 11:00pm) and assigned a new FTO. Cole Sorenson was always in teaching mode; he made sure I understood that it was his mission to teach and my mission to learn. I was to ask questions, seek information, and learn how to survive and thrive, while he taught me everything from tactical issues to report writing and more. His school of thought was that I would learn by doing, though in one particular instance, that was certainly not the case.

On one routine patrol, we stopped an individual who had an outstanding warrant; we waited for back-up, took him into custody, and transported him to the jail for booking. As a matter of protocol, Cole was required to remove his firearm and store it in a locker before entering the jail area. We completed the booking paperwork and then returned to patrol, but, unbeknownst to us, Cole had forgotten to retrieve his weapon and it did not become apparent until we made a traffic stop.

Now, a traffic stop may sound simple, but they are always unpredictable, potentially dangerous, and require being alert and following established procedures. Cole was very deliberate about how he conducted his approach to the vehicle: he checked for hidden risks and furtive movements, he stood where the driver had to look back to see him, and, per procedure, he moved his hand back to unsnap his holster and have his weapon within reach. Only at this point did we both simultaneously realize that he had no firearm. He shot me a horrified glance as I sat in the car. Fortunately, there was a shotgun in the front seat located in a special locked holding device. I quickly unlocked the device and positioned the weapon where I could use it, should it become necessary. Cole let the driver off with a warning and returned to the patrol car in short order, though when he saw me with the shotgun at the ready, we both had a good laugh. It was the kind of lesson Cole didn't have to teach me twice!

Finally, after two months of riding with Cole and nine months on the road by myself as a police assistant, I was given orders to attend the police academy, a three-month intensive training from sunup to sundown five days a week. I was raring to go!

My first day at the Phoenix Police Regional Training Academy started at 6:00 am, when the recruits gathered inside a Quonset hut that was used for a classroom. Our class included 10 or so candidates from Scottsdale, who were still civilian assistants, as well as officers from Phoenix P.D., the Maricopa County Sheriff's Office, and the police departments of several other cities and jurisdictions. We looked different from everyone else because we dressed in light blue uniforms, while they wore their badges, weapons, and full regalia. We carried no weapons throughout our training, unless we were assigned to be on the pistol range, which was one of many rules we were required to follow. It reminded me of Marine Corps Boot Camp. And I really felt a sense of belonging when I met Sergeant Ralph Griffith, a former Marine who was charged with overseeing our training and had a set of leather lungs that, to this day, still ring in my ears.

In the classroom, we were instructed on the Arizona Revised Statutes (Criminal Law and Traffic Law) and Constitutional Laws. But the majority of our time was spent on tactical and physical training. My favorite activity was the obstacle course: a sequence of walls, fences, cement tubes, and other obstacles designed to simulate potential scenarios encountered in the field. I had my own method for navigating the cement tubes: where I would run as fast as I could and then launch myself through a tube rather than crawl like the other recruits. One of the counselors, a Maricopa County Sheriff's Deputy, noted my adaptation and informed Sergeant Griffith that he thought it was unsafe. But, being the Marine that he was, Sergeant Griffith ruled that my methodology was an improvisation that worked for me and I was allowed to continue. Each time I ran the course, my teammates would watch in anticipation of my launch, slide, and recovery to running.

Because there was always some sort of team building activity designed to shape untried recruits into police officers, strong relationships were forged. I recall one day our class, known as "Griff's Griffins," returned to the academy grounds after an afternoon run, when we noticed one of our older classmates struggling to perform his required number of pushups. We gathered around him, and, while the staff member counted, we clapped our hands and cheered him on. With our encouragement, he passed that portion of his physical test, and it was this kind of teamwork that made me feel I was part of something special.

Upon graduation from the academy, I returned to the Scottsdale P.D. as a Police Assistant and was once again assigned to Team 3. Because I had already completed my training, time seemed to drag on as I attended briefings, took reports, investigated accidents, cataloged recovered property, directed traffic, and even shuttled the chief of police to and from the airport. About six months later, I was promoted to police officer!

This time, my FTO was Dale Deckley, who stood about 6'8" and had a dry, sarcastic sense of humor that was as biting as it was funny. Because of my short stature, it wasn't long before people started referring to us as "Mutt and Jeff." Our first shift together was July 4, 1979. Holiday or not, I couldn't wait to get to work that day because it was the beginning of my career as a full-fledged police officer. About midway through the shift, we were dispatched to a burglary in progress, and while it turned out to be a very generic arrest, I was beside myself with excitement. It was my first arrest! Dale and I debriefed every microsecond of the call from start to finish, and as I relived every moment, Dale was patient and complimentary of my tactical performance. He had to be exasperated, but he never let on. And for the next six weeks, he did everything he could to prepare me for the day I would be on my own, and I am grateful for the time we spent together.

Prior to my promotion, I had kept a pretty tight rein on my public consumption of alcohol, but once I became a police officer, it seemed more normal to drink and off came the restraints. After about six months on the force, I met an acquaintance at a local bar and we drank until closing time. He then suggested we go to his place to drink some more, so we got on our motorcycles around 1:00 am and wove our way through the streets of Scottsdale. My companion must have been really drunk, because he rode like a wild man, and, of course, a patrol officer witnessed his erratic behavior and gave chase. Not wanting to get into trouble, I quickly departed and went home, thinking I had gotten off scot-free. But then the phone rang. The officer questioned me about the other guy and I denied knowing him, which got me into the very trouble I was hoping to avoid. The consequence of my being dishonest led to a 10-day suspension from work without pay, which, in turn, led to me taking a good hard look at my drinking. And I was successful in stopping--for a while. I threw all my energy into being the best police officer I could be. I hustled and made lots of arrests, including an unusual one where I happened to be in the right place at the right time.

One evening while on patrol, a middle-aged woman driving east from Phoenix into Scottsdale flagged me down. I pulled in behind her, turned on the light bar, and as I approached her on the driver's side, I noticed a rifle in the back seat. Intuitively, I sensed something was wrong. Proceeding with caution, I asked her if she needed assistance, and she told me she had just shot her husband with that rifle! Now, I was still pretty new to police work, and this was a strange situation indeed. I asked her to step out of the vehicle, advised her of her Miranda rights, and, after making sure there were no other weapons in the car, asked her if she wanted to continue her account. She readily agreed.

The woman and her husband had spent the day drinking at a bar in Phoenix, when something sparked an argument, and it ended with the husband back-handing her off her stool. She calmly left, drove home, retrieved the rifle, and returned to the bar, where she waited in the parking lot. Her window of opportunity presented itself when, through an open side door, she could see her husband preparing to line up a shot at the pool table. She took aim and fired, hitting him in the groin.

Astonished with her openness about a very serious situation, I immediately notified my supervisor and requested dispatch contact Phoenix P.D. to see if they were working a bar shooting. They were, and an officer was sent to interview the primary suspect, whom I had managed to "apprehend!" I took the woman and her rifle to the station, had her vehicle towed, and when the Phoenix officer arrived, turned over the investigation to him.

My squad mates and supervisor razzed me for weeks about that arrest. As I recount instances like these, I realize that the camaraderie and bonding amongst police and public safety personnel is beyond description and like nothing else I have ever experienced. There is an acknowledgement and a knowing between those who perform this kind of work that can only be shared and understood by the ones who have done it. It is one of the reasons I was attracted to the work, along with the variety. Every shift is different: there is constant engagement and anything can and usually does happen.

At this point, things were going well for me, both professionally and personally. Karen and I were married in a beautiful ceremony at the Scottsdale Glass and Garden Church in 1980, and we lived rent free at our apartment because I acted as security at the complex. And at work, I already had my eye on what I wanted to do next.

Chapter 5

SPECIAL ENFORCEMENT UNIT

From the day I became aware of the undercover narcotics crew, I knew that was what I wanted to do. Often at the police station, I would see a particularly grungy looking character with long, stringy dark hair and a fu-man-chu mustache wearing shabby worn-out clothes, and he would walk through the station like he owned it, talking comfortably with uniformed officers. Wondering who this guy was, I asked around and found out his name was Joe, and he was on an undercover assignment. What undercover assignment? I didn't know much about these kinds of activities, but it sounded fascinating and I began contemplating the possibility of working undercover.

Then, one day while on routine patrol, I was contacted by the Team 3 commander, Captain Finch, which was unusual because commanders typically communicated through the chain of command, and he instructed me to meet with the Burglary Task Force to take custody of an individual and some stolen property. When I arrived at the location, I saw Joe, dressed as he always was, and a bunch of rough-looking guys I had never seen before who were similarly dressed. They greeted me and handed over the subject and the property. This was my first interaction with the Special Enforcement Unit (SEU), and as I observed their ease with and confidence in each other and their obvious commitment to the mission, my casual interest became a driving need to be part of this group.

Thereafter, every time I ran into Joe or the other guys, I talked them up and let it be known that I was ready, willing, and able to join the SEU. My chance finally came when I had been on the force about 5 years. In 1982, I was selected to become an undercover narcotics detective. I could not have been more excited. To prepare myself for my first day on the new job, I read books, I questioned other officers, and I let my hair grow out and didn't shave for a week! With my wife's admonishment to "Be careful and don't get hooked" taken to heart, my Smith & Wesson 9mm and my new flat badge case in my pocket, I walked out my front door, without any idea how my life was about to change.

Once I arrived at the SEU enclave, everything happened pretty quickly. After meeting Detective Bob Meirs, who I was assigned to, the other six members of the squad, the prerequisite joking about being the new guy, got out of the way and we got down to business. Detective Meirs explained that he had been working a case against a small-time drug dealer, who had sold cocaine to him on two occasions. His plan was to set me up as the "money man," and entice the guy to sell me an eighth of an ounce of cocaine. At that time, the law provided for an automatic five-year prison sentence for a drug sale in excess of $300, and since an eighth ounce sold for $350, it was an excellent opportunity to put a drug dealer out of commission. My training officer, a fellow Detective, called the guy and made arrangements for us to meet in about an hour.

On the way to our appointment with "Skip," the drug dealer in question, The Detective. briefed me on my story and we covered all the eventualities, but I was still incredibly nervous and hyped up, so we stopped at the grocery store and I bought a six pack of Killian's Red Beer. I drank a couple and that seemed to help calm me down. However, when we arrived and Skip got into the car, every fiber of my being was vibrating and my excitement was at a level that approximated when I used to play football. My adrenaline, mixed with an undercurrent of fear, was off the charts. I was certain Skip would make me a cop, but he didn't; he was simply interested in making the sale and getting the money. Then, he turned to me and offered me a "taste."

This was expected. People who sell drugs often want to see you do the drugs as a way of proving that you are not a police officer, but it was still a conundrum. Part of my questioning the other officers I mentioned earlier was about this very situation. According to experienced undercover operatives, there are a number of ways to fool the bad guys, including spilling the cocaine on the floor, pretending to smoke, or blowing through the straw to scatter the substance. However, the consensus was that at some point, no matter how hard you tried not to, you would have to do a little to keep from having your cover blown or worse, getting hurt or killed. So there, in the back seat of that car on October 17, 1982, I made the choice to "just do it." Prior to that date, I had never used cocaine. My experience with substances was limited primarily to alcohol and marijuana. The 80s were a time when cocaine was all the rage, a designer-type drug that all the hip, slick, and cool people used, and I guess I wasn't one of that crowd because until my first night of undercover narcotics work, I had never even seen the drug.

What happened in the next few moments is hard to put into words. The powerful forces of alcohol, cocaine, and adrenaline running through my body were like nothing I had ever experienced. It was both exhilaration and horror. My mind was racing with the thought, "This is amazing," but my spirit was screaming, "This is wrong!" Inside I was reeling, but on the outside, I had to present a cool façade to continue acting out my role in the sting.

We agreed on a price and I handed over the money with the pre-recorded serial numbers. We then watched Skip go into an apartment. This turned out to be a lucky break for us because it wasn't his apartment but rather that of his dealer, which meant we now had probable cause to believe our money and more drugs were inside. We contacted a judge and secured a search warrant. With the help of all our other team members, we surrounded the front and rear entrances to the apartment. I rang the doorbell, and when the door was opened, we forcibly entered, subdued the occupants, and began the search. And we found the mother-lode: drugs, paraphernalia, our money, and indicia of ownership.

Booking the suspects at the station, cataloging the evidence, and conducting interviews took until around midnight, and when I finally got home, I was too wound up to sleep. Karen and I had some of the best sex I can remember. I was high on my first undercover contact, a good arrest, a sense of accomplishment, great sex, and my new friend: cocaine. This new friend held promise. It beckoned me with its allure of excitement, freshness, and the pure physical pleasure that came with its use. I've heard it said that some people are hooked from their first taste, and that was certainly true for me. I ignored all the warning signals my belief system and my moral compass sent me, and I never once considered that I would become a slave to the drug or be a daily user, like the people I was working to put behind bars.

After my first undercover buy and trying cocaine for the first time the internal bomb went off and the beast was now out of the cage. I wasn't aware of it at the time because of the role of denial, but this train had left the station and I was strapped in for the ride. Years later, I would discover this missive at a 12-step meeting for cocaine addicts:

Dear Friend,

I've come to visit once again. I love to see you suffer mentally, physically, spiritually, and socially. I want to have you so restless that you can never relax. I want you jumpy and nervous and anxious. I want to make you agitated and irritable so everything and everybody makes you uncomfortable. I want you to be depressed and confused so that you can't think clearly or positively. I want to make you hate everything and everybody--especially yourself. I want you to feel guilty and remorseful for the things you have done in the past that you'll never be able to let go. I want to make you angry and hateful toward the world for the way it is and the way you are. I want you to feel sorry for yourself and blame everything but your addiction for the way things are. I want you to be deceitful and untrustworthy, and to manipulate and con as many people as possible. I want to make you fearful and paranoid for no reason at all and I want you to wake up during all hours of the night screaming for me. You know you can't sleep without me; I'm even in your dreams.

I want to be the first thing you wake up to every morning and the last thing you touch before you black out. I would rather kill you, but I'll be happy enough if I can put you back in the hospital, another institution or jail. But you know that I'll still be waiting for you when you come out. I love to watch you slowly going insane. I love to see all the physical damage that I'm causing you. I can't help but sneer and chuckle when you shiver and shake, when you freeze and sweat at the same time, when you wake up with your sheets and blankets soaking wet.

It's amazing how much destruction I can do to your internal organs while at the same time, working on your brain, destroying it bit by bit. I deeply appreciate how much you sacrifice for me.

The countless good jobs you have sacrificed for me. All the fine friends that you deeply cared for--you gave them up for me. And what's more, for the ones you turned against yourself because of your inexcusable actions--I am more than grateful.

And especially your loved ones, your family, and the most important people in the world to you. You even threw them away for me. I cannot express in words the gratitude I have for the loyalty you have for me. You sacrificed all these beautiful things in your life just to devote yourself completely to me. But do not despair my friend, for on me you can always depend. For after you have lost all these things, you can still depend on me to take even more. You can depend on me to keep you in living hell, to keep your mind, body and soul.

I WILL NOT BE SATISFIED UNTIL YOU ARE DEAD, MY FRIEND.

Faithfully yours,
Cocaine

These proved to be very prophetic words. Everything described in that letter came true for me. Addiction to any substance/process is without question cunning, baffling, and powerful. My addiction to cocaine and alcohol took me to the very gates of insanity and nearly to death's door itself. I am truly grateful to be alive, and grateful that I am clean and sober as I write these words.

I began to make some cases. I would go to the bars and troll for unsuspecting small-time dealers. All the time drinking alcohol and using cocaine; of course, I rationalized and justified these behaviors as being part of the job. I made some small cases. This actually led to being introduced to bigger players in the food chain. As each day, week, and month passed, I became more and more confident of my own ability, and more and more selfish, self-serving, and self-absorbed. I drank daily, used cocaine sporadically at first, but the beast was coming on and I never even saw it.

To convince drug sellers/dealers to sell drugs to me, I had to have a story--fictitious tale of who I was and why I wanted that person to sell drugs to me. In essence I had to lie.

The first time I had to really think quickly was during a cocaine buy in a Central Phoenix condo. I had met a young lad who graciously sold me some cocaine, and after about three sales of a gram each, I worked him up to an eight-ball. Which is 1/8 oz of cocaine. Now for this buy we conducted a surveillance of his partner leaving the condo and going to another location to get the drug. Apparently, during the trip over and back, the partner made the surveillance team and called back to the condo. I didn't know this at the time, but sensed something was amiss when the younger dealer began eyeing me suspiciously. The older one drove around quite a bit, in a counter surveillance measure; the surveillance team picked up that he apparently had made them so they backed off. Upon his return to the condo, both men confronted me about being a cop.

On the one hand, it was a frightening experience; but on the other hand, I really got off on the drama of the whole thing. Being in that position, knowing that I had to keep my wits about me to survive, was exciting. My adrenal glands had to have been wide open to full capacity. The shouting match in that condo was momentous. When they accused me of being a cop, I assured them that I was, in fact, the "chief of police." They demanded to see my driver's license, at which time I accused them of being cops. This dangerous game was certainly stimulating, exciting, and, I realize now, highly addictive.

I managed to back them both off and actually managed to convince them that I was not a police officer, that, in fact, I should be worried that someone was following them putting me in jeopardy of arrest. I apparently convinced them because I walked out of there that day, with the eight-ball of cocaine, and my life. I debriefed this situation with the rest of the teamothers from the position of being scared that they had discovered who I really was; I did not share how much I really enjoyed the game. I snorted some cocaine that night, and drank a lot of alcohol. This was some kind of job, and what a life!

We were next assigned to search for a man who was suspected of murdering a drug dealer in Scottsdale in the late 1970s. This suspect had been on the run for several years and information had been developed that he was back in the Phoenix area, on the lam. He was said to have found employment with a group that worked State Fair Midway rides. Thus, our entire unit was assigned to frequent the State Fair and attempt to locate and arrest this guy. The scene that is embedded in my mind is being on the Arizona State Fair Midway just as the Department of Public Safety officers had finished their daily briefing. The officers, who all appeared to be six foot or taller, were en masse leaving a tent to take their positions within the fairgrounds, to ensure security for the public. Their uniforms were freshly pressed, their patent leather gun belts gleaming, they were very visible and impressive. As I observed this scene unfold, I saw a small boy with his mother watching the officers. His eyes were glued to these men as they strode confidently past him and his mother with an occasional nod or tousling of his hair by these giant peacekeepers. Now as I stood there watching I was struck by the stark difference in their appearance and mine. I was in jeans and a t-shirt, bearded, wearing an earring, with long unkempt hair... yet we shared the same purpose. This was certainly a strange, new world for me. We spent several days at the fair in an attempt to locate and arrest the target for a homicide. After all this time we were unable to locate the suspect.

During my time in the SEU, our team was responsible for putting a lot of bad guys away and taking a lot of drugs off the street. I hadn't been in the unit very long when I was assigned a partner, Detective Meirs. He arranged to meet one of our confidential informants (CI's) at a bar in Scottsdale. Now, developing informants or "snitches" was tricky business because they all had their game and different reasons for collaborating with the police. Some were defendants working off their cases, some had a grudge against former associates and were willing to provide information, and some even had altruistic motives of ridding the community of drugs and the people who sell them. Working with CI's helped us make cases against street level dealers, with the hope of moving up the food chain to nail the higher-ups. This is what we were to do when Detective Meirs and I met our CI that evening.

We arrived at the bar for our meeting and while we were waiting, I got the nagging feeling that I had seen the female bartender before. Weeks before, the department had received a nation-wide bulletin with the names, photos, and identifying marks of two suspects: a male and female who were wanted in Oregon in conjunction with a series of felony offenses. I told Detective Miers that I thought this might be the woman on the wanted poster, and when he concurred, I engaged her in conversation and struck a deal to obtain some drugs, which would be delivered by her boyfriend (the other half of the wanted duo). A very fortuitous turn of events!

We notified our team members, who positioned themselves outside the bar, and once the target arrived, the trap was sprung and both were taken into custody. Our CI never did show up, but the evening was still a success. I even got a commendation out of it!

Many of our successful cases made use of a CI. One of the informants I had developed did business with a small-time methamphetamine dealer in South Phoenix, and he gave me an address to check out. After obtaining a warrant, we arrived en-masse and surrounded the house. It wasn't long before the male occupant was caught trying to flee through an open window, and the female occupant finally opened the front door and was secured.

We then began an extensive search. We did find marijuana, scales, baggies, sifters, and other accouterments for the processing, packaging, and sale of drugs, but no meth. Throughout the whole two-hour search, a small dog yapped constantly in the backyard. Frustrated and annoyed both by our failure to find meth and by the dog's unrelenting noise, we were close to giving up. Then, one of the officers remembered that as we entered the home, he observed a Cool Whip container being thrown out the window and the dog chasing after it. Bingo!

There, in the backyard, was the now chewed-up receptacle, with a plastic bag containing white powder lying in close proximity. My keen detective instincts immediately deduced that the teeth marks on the container belonged to the canine suspect, but when I tried to explain to him that ingesting meth could cause him serious harm, he never stopped yapping long enough to hear me! Even after we finished all our processing and returned to our vehicles parked on the street, that dog was still barking.

At home I was turning into a ghost. I used the excuse of having to work as a reason to be absent from home. I was drinking and using cocaine daily. I totally exploited the love and caring of the woman I married. Of course, while I was doing it I had no discernible sense of guilt, shame, or remorse. That came later in never ending waves. As it was happening I only thought of myself, how to create scenarios where I could drink alcohol and use cocaine. As I look upon this now the devastation that is addiction is chilling. Addiction affected every relationship that I had. I became a user of people, places, and things to the degree that all I ever thought about was myself and how I could hedonistically satisfy myself with alcohol and drugs.

Certainly the truth about addiction is that one is never satisfied. Chasing the dragon is a real concept. I was forever in search of the euphoria of that first high and no matter how much I drank or used, I could never have that initial experience again. Today I look at addiction as a dark, soul sucking, merciless, incapacitating cloud that colors every aspect of a person's life. At the time, I wasn't consciously aware of the impact my behavior had on those closest to me. My response to it then was to drink more and use more drugs in the hope that the feelings of guilt, shame, remorse, and sadness would subside. The alcohol and cocaine provided temporary relief from those uncomfortable feelings, and I could further distract myself by making more cases. Making more cases was a double bonus because it required me to think about something other than myself, and the horrible state my personal life was in; and in an underhanded way the process of making more cases provided me with more drugs to use. I became quite adept at that.

The more cocaine I did, and the more alcohol I drank the fuzzier my thinking got. Go figure huh. I met some guys from the Phoenix Police Department who were working an undercover case on a guy from Scottsdale. These guys were the real deal. They looked rough and I was really impressed with their knowledge, skill, and appearance. The one guy actually put himself off as a biker. He looked the part and I was very impressed. They actually had a small-time case on a drug dealer named "Ronny". They turned him over to me to work off his charge. This was the eventual undoing for me because Ronny, was once again arrested in 1986 for additional drug charges. He then offered me up as a way to walk out of his new charges. What a nasty business. Double crosses, dirty deals... in that world it truly is survival by attrition. My entire personality changed as a result of the daily use of cocaine and alcohol. I became so fearful that I truly believed that no one, absolutely no one in that world is trustworthy.

As I continued using cocaine daily, and consuming alcohol to sleep and to counteract the effects of the cocaine, my physical health deteriorated as did my slim hold on mental health. I can recall telling my wife that I wanted to quit working for the police and just become a "biker nomad." She just looked at me like I was from another planet. I was seriously considering this. There were several times that I just wanted to walk away from what my life had become.

The job became my way of sustaining my drug habit. I was making lots of cases, including drug raids. I was a master manipulator both externally, that is with people I made cases against, and internally with the police department. I never told the truth about anything. It got so bad that I was barely able to tell the truth from the lies. When we did raids, I always manipulated it so that I cataloged the cocaine we seized and was able to steal some each time to keep my drug habit going. The conflict inside of me was at times literally unbearable. I alienated friends, co-workers, and family. I was always out late at night, my wife did the smart thing and left several times. I rationalized this as just another part of the life of an Undercover Narcotics Detective; after all, it was only a phase, and I would make it up to her later. It was all bullshit. I simply used her and everyone else in my world to get what I needed or wanted.

As you can imagine, being undercover was extremely stressful. But every once in a while, a situation came along that lightened the mood. I had been with the SEU for about six months when Richard Craven came on board as the unit supervisor, and he had a stable of informants from his days as a field operative that still provided him with inside information. One day he asked me to call a CI named "Olivia," who had details about a school teacher dealing drugs. This made it imperative that we move quickly on the case, yet still ensure officer safety by gathering as much information as possible on the home's physical layout, weapons, and stash areas before the raid.

As we approached the home, there were no outward clues as to anything unusual inside. We were often creative about our entry into the homes we raided: sometimes we lured people out with a female undercover officer requesting assistance, or sometimes we created a commotion that would bring the occupants outside. All manner of ruses were employed to gain safe entry, and, in all cases, a tape recorder was used to document entry time, method, and other important evidentiary data. In this particular case, I simply rang the doorbell, and when the door opened, we all sprang forward and secured the man on the floor at gunpoint.

We then fanned out to search for additional occupants. As the other officers secured someone else in another room, I proceeded past the stack of floor-to-ceiling aquariums in the living room (which upon later inspection were found to house various species of poisonous and non-poisonous snakes, lizards, and reptiles) to the kitchen, where I heard the distinctive sound of a chair scraping across tile. With my 9mm drawn and ready, I heard movement in an adjoining room and ordered whoever it was to stop and come out. No response. The door was slightly ajar, and I could see several large, industrial sized garbage cans but no one lurking inside, so I kicked the door open. Unfortunately, I underestimated how hard I kicked, and the door slammed against one of the garbage cans and rebounded shut. Through the closed door, I again ordered the unseen subject to come out, and when there was no response, I gently opened the door, expecting at any moment to be rushed or be face-to-face with a deadly weapon.

What I wasn't expecting was the lone occupant staring back at me. It was the largest, ugliest lizard I had ever seen, standing on its hind legs with its front paws on the trash can rim hissing at me. I could have sworn it was 10 feet tall, weighed a thousand pounds, and nearly gave me a heart attack! I was frozen in place, expecting it to shoot flames at me like some mythical fire-breathing dragon, when my teammates finally deigned to come over and see what had scared me out of my wits.

Putting our collective brilliant minds together, we decided the best course of action was for me to shut the door, trapping the monster inside. How I was chosen to do the deed I don't know, but after some convincing, in the form of questioning my manhood, I advanced cautiously and managed to curb my fear long enough to pull the door closed, as peals of laughter from my teammates reverberated through the kitchen. Adding to the chaos were the hand-cuffed residents, who kept screaming not to hurt their pet lizard. What a zoo!

My teammates needled me for weeks about that bust. The joking served its purpose to help us keep our sanity in the midst of dangerous situations and the "secret" life we had to live as undercover officers. I learned how to protect my identity and basically lie about whom and what I was. And I did this while using alcohol and cocaine on a daily basis.

Chapter 6

COCAINE: MY PRIMARY FOCUS

*O*ver the next weeks and months, the insatiable desire for cocaine began to rule my life. My primary focus became how I could drink alcohol and use cocaine without anyone knowing, and my job became my way of sustaining my supply. The SEU was making lots of cases. And when we conducted raids, I would "volunteer" to catalog whatever drugs we seized and then steal some each time to support my 7-grams-per-day habit. I also entered into a destructive relationship with a known criminal to gain access to his supply chain.

RobertRonny was a small-time dealer that I met in the fall of 1982. He was turned over to me by Phoenix PD to work off his case, and he was eager to share information, so we started with a few "certification buys" to get him qualified as a CI. This meant I would search him prior to going into a potential buy, give him money, and wait for him to return with the appropriate amount of drugs. Through these controlled situations, I was able to create search warrant affidavits because his information was "verified."

Shortly thereafter we set up an operation against a marijuana dealer; Robert made arrangements to have him deliver a couple of pounds of pot to me at Robert's house, which was under surveillance by our entire squad. I was to turn down the deal so that we could follow the drugs and apply for a search warrant once we knew where the dealer was storing them. It came off like clock-work, and we turned several hundred pounds of marijuana. Robert and I were off and running!

He proved to be a wealth of information and the SEU made several cases based on the intel he provided. He also supplied me with cocaine regularly. We became constant companions, for I had deluded myself into believing that he was necessary to work cases, when, in fact, I really needed him to procure more cocaine.

My life began to unravel over the course of 1983. In my capacity as an undercover officer, I had to lie convincingly to protect myself, and I rationalized that it was just part of the job. But the lying became too easy, especially as the growing desire for more and more alcohol and cocaine overtook over my senses. I never told the truth. It got so bad that I was barely able to tell true from false, and the conflict inside of me, the double-life, grew unbearable. I alienated friends, co-workers, and family. For example, I had made it a habit to speak with my mom at least twice weekly; all of a sudden, I didn't have time for those phone calls. And when I did call her, I really wasn't present; I was just going through the motions.

My marriage became a farce. I spent my days and nights in search of drugs, and then used alcohol to bring me back down so I could sleep, and even then, there were times when I didn't sleep for days. I was a slave to my addiction. It affected every relationship I had. I became a total; all I thought about was myself. My whole being was reduced to finding drugs, lying about my behavior, finding more drugs, lying some more, and making a few arrests to make things appear better. I was completely out of control.

My mental health deteriorated to the point where I would think in grandiose terms: I thought I was invincible in my job, or I arrogantly told my supervisor that I was sure we knew all the drug dealers in Scottsdale. Because I was so confident in my own ability, I grew progressively more selfish, self-serving, and self-absorbed. In my mind, I had become a legend. Looking back now, the term "insufferably egotistical" seems an apt description. I thought I could pull the wool over everyone's eyes at work by always being "on," but truly, I was fooling no one but myself.

My wife certainly wasn't fooled. We were already living separate existences in the same house because of my obsession with the next fix, so she did the smart thing and went to stay with her parents for a while. I was not a good husband, friend, communicator, or provider, doing what I wanted, when I wanted without taking Karen into consideration. I recall one incident when she bought a truck without telling me and I was enraged, but the truth was she was unable to communicate with me because I had completely shut her out. I was rarely home, and when I did come home, it was to an empty house. I had sunk so low, no one could stand to be around me. I couldn't stand myself.

Drunk and high was how I spent most of my waking hours. When I went to bed in the wee hours of the morning, I would take out my 9mm and place it on the nightstand before passing out. Upon wakening the next afternoon, the ritual was always the same: I would reach for the pistol, cock the hammer, and place the barrel in my mouth. I wrestled with the thoughts that I was a criminal, a horrible husband, and a lousy employee trying to pretend I was respectable. My police badge mocked me. It was, on the one hand, a symbol that I had worth, yet, on the other hand, it was a reminder that I was not living up to the ideal it represented. I don't believe I really wanted to die, but I hated myself for what I had become and knew that I could not bear to live in the same manner anymore. This routine went on for months. After each daily struggle with the gun, I would snort more cocaine and everything would be alright for a while.

My parents were also concerned about me. I went for days, weeks, and even a month without contacting them, excusing my lack of courtesy with an attitude of self-importance: I was too busy to call or visit. I had an answer and an explanation for everything. I remember attending family functions at my mother and father's home in Scottsdale. I was always carrying cocaine and I would sneak into the bathroom lay it out on the sink counter and snort it up. As

I look back on it, I was totally out of control, yet I didn't know it then. I thought I was having fun. I had the illusion of control of my life and didn't even have the sense to know it was an illusion. Even to this day I have no idea how I was able to function well enough to fool those around me that I was doing my job. I know that I became an expert at finding cocaine, and that became the sole focus of my existence.

Today there is nothing more real to me than the idea that no human power is capable of relieving me of my addiction. It was absolutely essential for me to find a power greater than myself to deal with my addiction to alcohol and cocaine. Without help from my Creator, whom I choose to call God, the addiction kicked my ass at every turn. No mother's plea, no wife's anger, no employer's wrath was capable of neutralizing the all-powerful vortex that consumed my body, mind, and spirit until there was nothing more for me to lose. It is my fervent belief that nothing short of spiritual intervention was capable of relieving me of the hopeless condition of both my mind and body; this spiritual intervention was to come in a variety of forms later in my life. The Grace extended to me by my Creator is beyond any words I can muster, and as I write these words today I am eternally grateful for that Grace.

Surprisingly, I was still able to function, albeit poorly. I tried to distract myself from my world gone awry by making cases. One of the arrests I made was a gangly, goofy kid named Jimmy K., who became a CI. In return for dropping his charges, he helped me make several cases against other dealers. In my fine-tuned state of mind, I reasoned it would be a good idea to introduce him to "Ronny" so that they could go into business together. This was another indication of how muddled my thinking had become. I knew they were selling drugs, but I not only did not stop them, I actually enabled them. I had completely lost sight of the reason I had joined the SEU. Eventually, Jimmy K. was indicted and was given a walk for his testimony against me at my trial.

Another CI that I ran was Naomi, who owned an escort service and, as a consequence, knew a lot of drug users and dealers. We had made several cases together, when a couple of odd twists occurred. First, my supervisor requested a meeting with her, and something, I'm not sure exactly what, developed between them. Second, one night I witnessed Naomi and one of our radio dispatch girls at a coffee shop conversing in a familiar way. It turned out that the dispatcher was an employee of the escort service, and was tipping off Naomi about law enforcement efforts to infiltrate her business.

In time, they were both arrested. But prior to that, I had confided in Naomi about a "drug run" I did with Ronnie to Boca Raton, Florida, where I hid a package of cocaine in my luggage (airport security procedures were different in those days) and transported it back to Phoenix. If my brain hadn't been so addled, I would have understood that I was giving information that could be used against someone who might have reason to use it in just that way. But I didn't, and that is just what eventually happened.

My poor performance at work finally caught up with me, and in January 1984, I was transferred out of SEU, after only about a year and one-half, back to patrol. A couple of months later, on April 12, I came to work with a gram of cocaine in my vial and bullet cap, a bullet cap was a tool used to snort cocaine right out of the vial, without having to lay it out in a line. (I had hollowed out the chamber so that it held more of a dose), when the Watch Commander met me in the hallway and informed me I was being administratively suspended. A shock of fear ran through me, as I thought of the drugs I had stashed. But much to my relief, the concern was about Naomi, her relationship with my sergeant, and the radio dispatcher. Supposedly, the Phoenix PD only wanted to ask me some questions, and, until the matter was cleared up, I was suspended. However, during my interviews, I was so afraid of losing my job and going to jail, that I did not tell the truth. The result of that particular lack of good judgment was a drop in pay.

The investigation progressed and I was subpoenaed to testify before a Grand Jury. As I sat outside the jury room, I looked over at my sergeant who was lying on a bench with his arm over his eyes, and I remember thinking how pathetic he looked. While I was inside, Naomi passed me a note proclaiming we would all have a party once this was over. I was mortified. What a mess my life had become!

Even with this soap opera unfolding before me, it didn't make me stop using cocaine, though I did slow down, thinking that if I just achieved the appropriate balance, I could stay sharp. So, out of necessity, I became an expert chemist by ingesting just enough cocaine to keep me functioning mentally, but not so much as to affect my physical health, with the proportionate amount of alcohol to keep me level headed. Now it is quite laughable all the machinations I went through to preserve the impression that everything was fine, but, at the time, it made perfect sense to the addict in me.

One oddity that occurred during this time was a previous CI I had used to make cases contacted me out of the blue. He didn't have any new information, nor did he express any interest in reestablishing our arrangement: he simply wanted to talk. This guy was working for the DEA to develop information about me, and was asking me questions about my activities within SEU. Later, I read investigative reports that he was working for the Drug Enforcement Agency (DEA) in the case against me, which I was completely unaware of at the time, and had provided details of our conversations.

The stress of managing my drug habit, the investigations, my rocky marriage and precarious family relationships became overwhelming. I knew that I had to make a change if I wanted to survive. It was no easy feat, but in early 1984 I stopped using cocaine and detoxified myself at home by drinking lots of gin and tonics, and, eventually, I was even able to taper off the alcohol. My mind became clearer. I started running every day and eating well, and, consequently, my physical health dramatically improved. I was a man on a mission to earn back the respect of my colleagues by working hard to restore their faith in me, becoming a top producer in terms of answering the most calls and making the most arrests.

Command Staff took notice and reinstated my pay. My wife took notice, and while we still had issues to work out, our relationship began to heal. In 1985, I was invited to play football for the Department of Public Safety team, and as part of my physical preparation, I made the choice to stop drinking. Things were really getting better. And no sooner than I had realized that everything was starting to look up, it all started coming back down again when it became necessary for me to shoot and kill a man in the line of duty.

Chapter 7

IF YOU TOUCH THE
GUN I'LL KILL YOU

*V*alentine's Day 1986 turned out to be a day I will never forget – for all the wrong reasons. I had been sober about 75 days and was working as a patrol officer on the day shift when I responded to a "hot tone." A hot tone is a warning signal from radio dispatch that alerts all police units to stop and listen carefully, as important information is about to be disseminated. The announcement was about a "man with a gun" at a residence in North Scottsdale. All the other North Patrol Units were occupied, so even though it was only a half hour before the end of my shift, I was assigned the call. The only other available unit to be assigned was a police detective, which is quite unusual, for a couple of reasons. First, detectives typically do not respond to these types of calls because they are in plain clothes and unmarked vehicles, and second, multiple units would normally respond to an emergency. In this instance, we were on our own.

Not being too far away when the call came in, I arrived in the neighborhood first. But the house numbers were so disjointed that I ended up right in front of the residence, which in terms of officer safety is not recommended because it put me in the kill zone, which puts me in a position to be injured, or killed, and gave me no opportunity to make a cursory threat assessment. I quickly backed up my vehicle as the detective sped by me in his, obviously also confused by the numbering system. By the time he made a U-turn and parked, I had already gotten out, placed my baton in my belt, and was scanning for activity. All I knew at this stage was that the suspect was the son of the homeowners and that he allegedly had a gun.

Then, a man emerged from the south side of the house, walked toward me, indicated the front door on the north side and said, "He's over there." I looked in the direction he was pointing and saw no one, so I asked, "Is he your son and does he have a gun?" As he turned away, he confirmed that his son did indeed have a gun. Once I heard this, I immediately retreated behind a 4-foot cement pillar at the edge of the pavement leading to the carport. In the meantime, the detective had made his way to the driveway, and upon hearing our exchange, withdrew to his vehicle parked on the other side of the street.

Once I was "safely" ensconced behind the pillar, I saw the suspect with his gun in his right hand pointed to the sky. I yelled, "Drop the gun" at least twice (though it may have been more), at which point, he brought down his arm and aimed his .25 caliber semi-automatic at me. Now, to my heightened state, it looked to be about the circumference of a trash can. It didn't matter that I had a 9mm and was proficient in how to use it; all I knew at that moment was that he was standing 15 yards away with the barrel leveled at me. Then he screamed, "Go ahead, motherfucker, kill me" and charged at me full steam ahead.

Now, if this had been a movie, it would have shifted into slow motion: the villain running dead on towards the good guy, who would have had no choice but to defend himself by shooting the suspect before he himself could be shot. And killing someone in the movies seems so straightforward, because the bad guys get what they deserve and everyone applauds. But, unfortunately, this was a real life-and-death situation and there was no director to yell, "Cut" before anyone got hurt. I had mere seconds to decide how this would play out, and I chose to rely on my training, police procedure, and my own common sense. I fired, and I kept firing until he quit coming at me. When the bullets hit his body, his momentum caused him to whirl around in a full pirouette, like a boxer taking a knock-out punch to the chin, before he landed face down on the driveway with the gun still in his hand.

It took 4 shots to take him down. The instant he fell, the shrieking started (and no, it wasn't me).

From inside the house, his mother began a high-pitched wail that momentarily distracted me from focusing on the body, which was when the father approached, knelt down and reached for the gun. I ordered him to step away, saying, "If you touch that gun, I'll kill you!" Then, the detective appeared and kicked the gun out of reach. In accordance with protocol, I removed the portable radio from my belt to call in a report that shots had been fired and that we needed a police supervisor and medical personnel to respond. But the detective interrupted my transmission and told me not to say anything; his reasoning for that continues to be unknown to me. I learned later that by stopping my report mid-sentence, the radio dispatch team thought I had been injured.

At this point, shock began to set in and I was functioning on auto-pilot: checking the body and administering first aid, locating the gun that had been kicked away, addressing the neighbors' concerns, informing the additional responders to the scene of the events that transpired. I moved about in a daze, not even realizing that the seam of my trousers had ripped down my left leg until one of the firefighters asked me if I was ok and then insisted on examining me from head to toe. While I stood there, the sequence of events played over and over again in my mind, and I recalled from my time at the academy that it was good to write down any details and any utterances made by those involved in situations like these. So, when the medic released me, I drifted over to my vehicle, retrieved a notepad and wrote down, "Go ahead, motherfucker, kill me." This notation was later offered into evidence at my trial.

More people continued to arrive on scene, including my good friend, Gene Richards, who was there in a supervisory capacity because my sergeant had the day off. The first thing he did was come over to me and said, "How are you doing, kid?" He instinctively understood how scared I was and just by that small gesture of concern, I felt my unease dissipate. He made sure I had everything I needed before securing the scene and directing the other officers in their duties, and his presence that day was a tremendous blessing and a good reminder that God often sends people to comfort and support us when things seem the darkest.

The preliminary investigation continued and it was suggested that I return to the station, but I couldn't drive my car back because the CSI team still needed to process it. Officer Craig was assigned to transport me. For some reason (the front seat was filled with gear or someone else was riding with him), I was told to get in the back. Unaware of the significance, I started to do what I was told when Gene came racing over and emphatically declared that I was not to be put in the back seat of that police car. In a heartbeat, I was seated in the front, but more importantly, it had been made abundantly clear to everyone at the scene that Gene believed I had acted appropriately and that I was to be treated with respect.

The ride back to the station provided a brief respite from the chaos of the crime scene, only to be replaced by an exhausting series of interviews. To prepare for the first one, I was taken to the interrogation room where people who are suspected of committing crimes are questioned. That made me a bit nervous: were my actions under suspicion?

After a short while, Police Chief Mike Gannon stopped by, patted me on the back, and offered his encouragement. As the waiting continued, I asked to call my wife. She, of course, said she would be right down, and, secretly, I felt a palpable relief knowing she would be there to support me. Once she arrived, we hugged and talked and cried, sharing some tender moments in the midst of a nerve-wracking situation. But I needed to focus on the upcoming interview, so I reluctantly sent her home while I waited for a representative from the County Attorney's Office.

They sent Mr. Joe Fuller, and some other investigators. We initially just talked about background stuff, such as my time in the Marine Corps and how long I had served on the Force. He shared that he also had been a Marine, which helped me relax a bit. Eventually, we walked through the entire scenario from start to finish, and one of the questions that really stood out to me was when he asked if I had been afraid for my life. I remember envisioning that young man yelling and running directly at me with his gun pointed and I told Joe that I had never, ever been more certain that I was going to die. After a few more follow-up questions, I asked Joe if I was going to be alright on this deal. His next words and all they convey can only be understood by those who have experienced the Marine brotherhood: in a tone of complete authority he answered, "Semper Fi."

The next interview was with several members of the department, including the chief of detectives and the chief forensic officer. They advised me that, as per standard operating procedure in a shooting case, I would be placed on administrative leave, my weapon would be impounded and I would be issued another. They also told me I could have as much time off as I needed. Not fully realizing the magnitude of my emotional turmoil, I asked only for the next day off.

At that point, all I wanted to do was go home. Several people stopped me as I made my way through the station, to the locker room and out into the parking lot. They all offered their support, but I felt a distinct difference in the way they perceived me. Perhaps it was just my own perception of myself that was playing tricks on me, but there was no disputing I had just killed someone and I would never be the same, never think of myself the same way or be the same in anyone else's eyes. I was forever changed.

Karen was waiting up for me when I finally got home. She had the television on and had been anxiously awaiting any news or more details about the incident. I wasn't paying much attention to the newscast until I heard them say, "Police gun down a man in his driveway: complete story at ten." Gunned down? Did they think I just gunned down an innocent man for no reason? It made me so angry to hear the most agonizing, frightening moment in my life reduced to a misleading statement void of the extenuating circumstances. My anger gave way to tears and I held Karen and let the story pour out of me. I didn't want to kill that guy! I just wanted him to put the gun down and stop threatening me. I had no choice!

Several years later, it was revealed that the suspect had been to rehab numerous times. When I encountered him, he had recently been released and had gotten drunk and attempted suicide. Some people speculated that in his extreme drunkenness, he was unable to seat the magazine into the weapon, therefore botching his attempt to take his own life. By pointing his gun at a police officer, he knew he would be killed. How tortured he must have been! This, however, was no comfort to me.

It did help that night when Karen told me how many people had called to express their concern, including Scottsdale mayor Herb Drinkwater. I called him back and he was quite effusive in his praise for a job well done and his thankfulness that I had not been injured. Then he said something that chilled me to the bone: he had heard that I had "cleaned up quite a bit" since my days in SEU. My heart dropped to my knees. I tried to hold it together as we finished our conversation, but my mind was racing. How did he know? How much did the department know, and what would they do about it?

Chapter 8

MY ARREST

My ordeal was just beginning. After a virtually sleepless night, I awoke the morning after the shooting to the thud of the newspaper hitting the driveway. Why I was anxious to read the accounts of what happened I don't know, but I devoured the news. Headlines and articles reported that the poor innocent suspect just wanted to hand his weapon to a police officer, when, with no provocation, he was shot in cold blood. The department's generic statement that the subject waved the weapon in a "menacing" manner was no better. I so wanted to pump my fist in the air and shout, "He aimed his gun and ran at me!"

But for the most part, my friends and co-workers were truly supportive. They were offended on my behalf when I was reassigned to station duties as I waited for the County Attorney's Office to review the incident and determine whether criminal charges should be filed. One of my newly assigned tasks was to load bullets into plastic baggies to distribute to officers during live fire training exercises. To me, this mindless chore was a temporary reprieve from my emotional roller coaster. But to my colleagues, it was busy work and beneath my dignity.

However, it didn't last long. On a Friday afternoon in early March, the patrol commander called me with the news that the shooting panel agreed my actions were appropriate to the menace present. And after reassuring my squad leader that I was good to go (suffering no hesitancy or lack of confidence in my ability to do the job), he suggested I remain on Team 3 but move to a southern beat. I accepted and was scheduled to be back on the road the next week. What a relief!

It was such a relief, that I decided a celebratory drink was in order. After all, I hadn't had a drink in over 3 months and if there was ever a time I deserved one, this was it! My favorite bar and my old drinking buddies welcomed me back with open arms, plying me with free drinks and helping me make up for lost time. Being the courteous guy I am and not wanting to let them down, I drank everything they bought for me. And so the flood gates opened and I willingly went back down the path of drinking daily.

A few weeks passed. I got back into the routine, enjoying being together with the rest of the squad, responding to calls, including one disturbance where a woman identified me as "the guy who murdered that kid," and even being sent out on a "man with a gun" call. And my old friend, Ronnie, with whom I had established a drug relationship, contacted me, hoping to get reacquainted. It turned out that it wasn't his idea to meet up. He was wearing a wire and working with the police to get me to admit I was involved with him in the distribution of cocaine.

Unbeknownst to me, at the time of the shooting, I was being investigated by the Drug Enforcement Agency (DEA), which, in hindsight, accounted for some of the tension with the Command Staff during the aftermath, and the comment the mayor made to me on the phone.

But I was blissfully unaware, going about my business as usual, thinking life was pretty good. The shooting situation was behind me, Karen was pregnant, and we were temporarily staying at my parents' while our new house was being built. I remember pondering as I got up early for a 7 am briefing on Good Friday, March 28, 1986, that I loved my job and it was going to be a great day. I shaved, showered, ate a quick breakfast, kissed my sleeping wife goodbye, and drove to work whistling a happy tune.

When I arrived at the station parking lot, both the chief and the assistant chief's cars were already there, and I wondered if something had happened during the night that caused them to respond. Then, the voice of one of my squadmates snapped me out of my reverie and we made small talk as we walked to the door and punched in the combination.

The door opened and all hell broke loose. A lieutenant put his hand on my chest and shoved me against the wall. Several others then surrounded me, searched me, and escorted me to the booking room, where, thankfully, a curtain had been drawn. At least the "fishbowl effect" of having everyone at the station witness the fingerprinting and photographing process, as well as my humiliation, was minimized. None of those who effected the arrest said anything to me, or attempted to ask me any questions.

As I stood behind the booking counter, so scared I could hardly breathe, a part of me was relieved that the hiding, lying, and deceit were finally over. My past misdeeds had caught up with me, and there was nowhere to run: I was under arrest for conspiracy to distribute narcotics and obstruction of justice. A wave of shame washed over me. The only bright spot in an otherwise degrading experience was when the County Attorney arrived and assured me that my wife, who I had taken on a drug run with Ronny to Florida pretending it was a vacation, was not a target of the investigation. I was to learn later that Ronny had been arrested for distributing cocaine and had given me up to the authorities in exchange for a "walk" on his charges.

After booking, we walked over to the Justice Court for my initial appearance. The judge, who I had testified before numerous times and presented affidavits for search warrants in my capacity as an undercover narcotics detective, was shocked to see me. I felt my face flame with embarrassment and nearly lost my composure. One of the purposes of the initial appearance is to determine release options for the defendant, for which the County Attorney requested a $50,000 bond. The judge then offered me a chance to speak. So, with as much eloquence, humility, and respect as I could muster, I explained why I should be released on my own recognizance. I outlined my employment history, my ties to the community, expressed my pride about becoming a father in a few months, and rambled on and on trying to impress upon her that I was an upstanding citizen and certainly not a flight risk. When I was done, she set my bail at $165,000. I was in the process of learning a valuable lesson; my first thoughts and words are not necessarily the best.

Castigating myself for not just keeping my mouth shut, we returned to the Police Department and I called home. If I thought speaking in front of the judge was tough, it was nothing in comparison to having to tell my mom that I had been arrested. The disgrace I had brought on my family, my department, my profession, and myself nearly drowned me. Of all the things I went through, the disgrace that I had brought to myself and others was perhaps the most difficult thing for me personally to resolve. Tears threatened. I hung up and swallowed hard to not break down. Just then, a female Warrant Detail Officer, who was a friend, entered the booking room, playfully kneed me in the leg, and laughed. It buoyed my spirit.

Next, two detectives drove me to the Maricopa County Jail with my hands in cuffs (in front rather than in back after I convinced them I would not try to escape or hurt them), and was booked into a pod that housed men awaiting trial. It was an open style room with a television that, to my dismay, was broadcasting a video of me being led to and from court and in and out of the transport vehicle. There was my image for everyone at the jail to see. This put me in serious danger; so within a few hours, I was transferred to a solitary cell for my own protection. I remained there for three days.

In the meantime, my parents had hired Joe Chornenky to represent me and had posted the bond for my release by putting up their house to guarantee my appearance in court. After I returned home, I met with Joe to review the evidence against me, but I couldn't concentrate. Here I was, about to enter the battle for my future, and all I could think about was how much I had screwed up, what a loser

I was, and how it might be easier on my family and better for me if I just ended my life. While my attorney was showing me documents, I was picturing myself plunging a big kitchen knife into my chest (my guns had been confiscated as a condition of my release). When I finally realized the folly of where my thoughts had taken me, I excused myself from our meeting and called an old friend.

Pat M., who was a regular customer at my father's tavern, used to stay with my sister and me when we were young while my parents worked late at the bar. After years of heavy drinking, he joined a 12-Step group, got sober, and trained to become a certified counselor. We had had sporadic contact over the years. But while I was in jail, he called and left a message for me, saying, "For as many people as there are pointing a finger at you, there are that many and more praying for you." I knew I could call this man and tell him what I was thinking. He was working as a plumber at the time and was on the job when I phoned, but after making me promise not to hurt myself before he got there, he dropped everything and came over.

Spending the day with him had a profound effect on me. We talked, ate lunch, worked, and talked some more, as he shared his experience, strength, and hope with me and got me over the hump. His caring proved to me that I was not worthless, and that taking responsibility for my actions was the choice a man who had pledged to serve his country as a Marine and serve his community as a police officer would make. He was right. He turned out to be right about many things.

Chapter 9

I'LL DO ANYTHING TO
GET OUT OF THIS

Pat was right that I needed help. He was right that I needed to attend some kind of treatment program, and my lawyer, Joe, heartily agreed. There was a lot of evidence against me, and the county attorney was pushing for prison time, so about the only option left if I hoped to get a favorable sentence was to prove I was seriously seeking rehabilitation. So I signed up for the $15,000 treatment program at a local treatment provider, not because I wanted to get sober, but because I thought it would help my case.

My initial session was scheduled for a Monday morning, but after a few days of reading in the newspaper about myself and the awful things I had done and seeing my image on television, I was so overcome with guilt and shame that I couldn't face a bunch of accusing, judgmental strangers. Monday came and went, and I did not show up. When Joe called to see how it went and I admitted to blowing it off, he hit the roof. He commanded me to high-tail it to the group the next day because it was essential to our defense, and he wasn't concerned with whether I felt like going or not. His tirade worked: I went the next day, and the next, and the next. For two months, I was in treatment three hours a day, five days a week.

My first day was the hardest. Just the simple act of identifying myself to the receptionist was difficult because then she would know who I was and what I had done. Once the paperwork was complete and I had undergone a physical and provided blood and urine samples, I was directed to the gathering. As I entered the room with chairs forming a circle and several people milling about, I thought to myself, *I can't believe I'm even here, let alone expected to bare my soul to these losers.* It was bound to be excruciating, and I almost turned around to make a quick getaway. But one of the guys saw me, made direct eye contact, and said, "Welcome to the group." I was stuck.

Upon the arrival of the leaders—Warren B., a slight man of 5'6" who wore an eyepatch and favored white, long-sleeved shirts, and Laura C., a middle-aged Hispanic woman—everyone took their seats. I sat down, wishing I was anywhere but there. Putting on my best happy face, I tried to appear calm, but I was angry, afraid, and resentful, and at the same time the slightest bit hopeful that somehow I could get out of this. But it wasn't to be.

The leaders introduced themselves, pointed out that I was a newcomer, and invited everyone else to introduce themselves. Each took his or her turn. By the time they finished, I knew which ones were alcoholics, drug addicts, or both; their drug of choice; how long they'd been clean and sober; and how long they'd been a member of the group, as well as a lot of other personal details they felt compelled to share with me. As this was going on, I was listening with one ear and wondering who in their right mind would be so forthcoming with such damning information. Were they crazy? Was this what I was supposed to do: divulge my deepest shame and darkest secrets to people I'd never met before, all in the name of therapy? All eyes turned to me with visible expectation. So, with my arms folded tightly across my chest, jaw tilted upward, and eyes focused on no one in particular, I choked out that my lawyer thought it was a good idea for me to attend, but that I wasn't an alcoholic or addicted to anything. I laid my belligerent denial on them good and thick.

There were knowing smiles and darting glances to each other around the circle, for every single one of the other participants had in some way, on some level, experienced the same thing on their first day: fear, powerlessness, unwillingness to admit they had a problem. So I'm sitting there in fear, totally powerless over my addiction and the consequences of being addicted, and all the while unwilling to admit that I had a problem. This is by its very definition a problem, and I wasn't even smart enough to know that. But each and every one of those who had started before me knew that I was addicted, that I didn't know it, and therefore I was living in denial. What I didn't understand until later was that they meant me no harm; they simply had more knowledge and experience than I did.

The agenda moved on to reading from some reflection books on how to gain perspective on the events and circumstances that occur in our daily lives, and from there to an open discussion by the individual group members. All manner of topics came up, some having to do with addictions, but mostly issues related to everyday living, such as marital relationships, job stress, self-image, and so forth. Some of my defenses began to soften, and I became seduced by how comfortable these courageous people were in disclosing the personal aspects of their lives. As of yet, I had no such courage. The next time it was my turn to talk, I lied.

During a lull in the interaction, Warren commented in a curious and very non-threatening way that he had expected me to have started the group the day before. Well, I was not about to admit the real reason, so I spun a tall tale about having a flat tire. The threat I perceived was squashed, and the group's attention diverted, but surprisingly, I felt no triumph. My dishonesty left me with a sour taste.

Midway through the morning we took a break, and the smokers congregated in the front of the building to light up. I attempted to distance myself from them by standing apart, but apparently once you are part of the group, you are fair game for an overture of friendship.

The first young man to approach me was Jeff, who put me on instant alert by stating, "I thought I recognized you." He proceeded to assure me that no one was judging me and that this was a safe place to deal with our self-destructive habits. That took some of the starch out of my spine.

We were then joined by Matt, a kid of no more than 21, who exclaimed, "Man, I never thought I would see a cop here!" He continued by saying he admired my fortitude for getting treatment and that he realized what a tough position I was in. I was nearly speechless. Never once had I entertained the idea that I would be accepted for who I was and what I had done or that I would be free to talk about it with people who understood, but here the first day is not yet over, and these two made me feel safe.

The feeling continued through the rest of the session. At the end, Warren asked if I would meet with him afterwards, and all my instincts told me this was a man I could trust. Perhaps it was his quiet confidence or his ability to put one at ease, but I had no more than sat down when my whole story just poured out. Other than the facts of my case, which my attorney had instructed me not to reveal, I confessed my fear, guilt, shame, and sincere remorse, and at no point did I sense he was judging me. He did not flinch or recoil. He simply listened. For me, it was the release of a burden I had carried for years.

The next day, I arrived early at the treatment center and actually looked forward to seeing Jeff and Matt. We smoked cigarettes and drank coffee, and I could feel myself becoming part of something special, something that made me considerably less defensive and was instrumental in turning my intense self-hatred into an examination of the behaviors that got me into trouble in the first place.

About halfway through the morning session, I decided to take a risk and admit why I was really there, although I couldn't yet acknowledge being an addict. I told them I was a police officer who had been arrested and charged with narcotics offenses, that I was terrified of going to prison, that my wife was pregnant with our first child, and that I had recently shot and killed a man in the line of duty. When I finally ran out of words, I hung my head, expecting but not wanting to see their judgment, shock, and obvious disgust. Instead, they showered me with acceptance and praise for my willingness to tell the truth and formed a figurative fortress of support around me. For all their own issues of alcoholism, drug addiction, codependency, or whatever brokenness had brought them to the group, they enveloped me with the fullness of their compassion.

Something changed in that moment. I had passed some sort of test by opening up and engaging in the treatment process, and I felt an unexpectedly close bond to this group whom I had known for less than 48 hours. This was a good beginning, but there were many more miles to travel on my road to recovery.

Another phase of my treatment, which was to run concurrently, started when Warren handed me a packet of written materials. This packet contained information on family roles, the "Big Book," which is the basic text of Alcoholics Anonymous, and a Community-wide 12-Step Meeting Schedule. I asked what all this stuff was. Warren informed me that regular attendance at 12-Step meetings was required by the program and it was at these meetings that I would find recovery. I soon learned that 12-step meetings were actually free of charge. Now, I might not be the brightest bulb in the pack, but it was not lost on me that it cost money to go to treatment, but recovery was free!!! My sponsor (an AA member who has worked through, and applied the steps of the program in his life)and I have worked on that one to free me of that pseudo-resentment.

Anyway, getting me to 12-Step meetings is where my friend Pat came in. As I already mentioned, he was a rock those first few days after my arrest, and came to mean even more to me in the months before my trial. Pat used to drink at my dad's tavern, and sometimes, when my parents were working weekends at the bar, he and his wife would watch my sister and me. I didn't have much contact with him through high school, my time in the Marines, and during college, though I did see him once in a while at my folks' house. We would share a few drinks, a few laughs and a few stories.

Eventually, he got sober by working the 12 Steps. Now he called to tell me people were praying for me. We started spending more and more time together, with him continually challenging me to attend a 12-Step meeting. I finally capitulated and will never forget my first experience.

Chapter 10

RECOVERY STARTS

I had not had much contact with Pat after high school. I did see him once at a party at my parents' home when I was home on leave from the Marines. The two of us drank and shared some stories of what it meant to be home on leave. I had no idea then how much influence this man would have on my life.

As I mentioned, Pat was a plumber, but after getting sober through the 12 Steps he began working on becoming a certified counselor.

After my arrest, while I was in the Maricopa County Jail, I called my parents. My mom told me that Pat had called and left a message for me. I have never forgotten that message: "For as many that are pointing fingers at you, there are that many praying for you." That message has meant more to me as the years passed. I have clung to that in times of trial. In the days that followed my release from jail, I sought Pat out, and spent lots of time, alone, and with him at 12 Step meetings. I cannot begin to express enough gratitude for Pat's work with me before, during, and after my prison experience.

I attended my first 12 Step Meeting with Pat in April 1986, after my release from jail. Pat had challenged me to attend a meeting with him, and I had given him every excuse that I could think of to avoid doing so. Eventually I went to a meeting with him, and I will never forget my experience; I was scared to death, but I met some very interesting people at that first meeting. This first group that I would attend was to meet in an airplane hangar; we met in central Phoenix and drove over in Pat's car. Once we arrived, we walked from the car to an isolated hangar where the meeting was to occur. Standing outside the hangar was a man who simply looked like someone had taken a refrigerator and put a head on it. This guy was enormous. He walked up to us and acknowledged Pat, and when Pat introduced me to Kendall he reached out with both arms, hugged me and said "I love you, and I'm glad you're here." Now I was already very nervous about attending a 12 Step Meeting, after this greeting I was terrified. What was this meeting about? And what about all this hugging stuff? And another male just told me he loved me! This was not what I was looking for, not what I thought a 12 Step Meeting should be.

I had so many preconceived notions about 12 Step Meetings--none of them based in fact. I heard little about the program that night because I was unable to hear a word anyone said. I kept my eyes glued to Kendall, and was devising a plan to deal with him should he decide to come over to where I was sitting and try to hug me again. There were about a dozen people at the meeting, mostly middle aged men. They laughed and had a sense of ease about them that was attractive; at the end of the meeting they formed a circle, held hands, and said The Lord's Prayer. They invited me to stand and pray with them, and to my extreme shame I was the only one person in that group who did not know the words to that prayer. Through tears I watched as they comfortably bowed their heads and prayed with each other. I felt so low and filled with self-loathing, and they knew it, but they let me stand with them anyway. They encouraged me to come back, learn more, and not drink. I was reeling, filled with shame, fear, self-hatred, and a sense that I was utterly worthless. None of my feelings had anything to do with anything they said or did; I simply knew that I had reached rock bottom. I was lost; I knew nothing; I believed completely bankrupt as a human being with nothing of value to contribute. Yet even in that moment these people welcomed me, shook my hand, hugged me, and invited me to come back. This was going to be a strange ride for sure.

While the first meeting touched me in a spiritual way, the second one was much different in that I truly thought I was going to die, in a very real physical sense, at that very meeting. I met Pat again, in West Phoenix, and we set out in search of a meeting called Shikkers. I have no idea why they called it that. Pat explained that it was a meeting primarily for newcomers. We went to several different locations searching for this meeting, and I remember thinking that this was certainly a strange way to provide meetings for people who needed them. Keep in mind that I was not at all convinced that I was an alcoholic; I was simply curious as to how these people could be so calm, happy, and focused and call themselves alcoholics. Also, I could be amongst them, and they did not have to know anything about me, which was, of course, very attractive to me.

We finally found the meeting at a local church. We walked into a room full of at least 200 people. I was amazed that so many people would be gathered for a 12 Step Meeting. What happened next chilled me to my very core. I looked up to the front of the room and observed a very tall, heavy set, bearded man speaking to this large crowd. He had a commanding presence that spoke of former military, and he was definitely in charge. Pat and I found a table in the center of this large room and settled in just as the man, whom I later learned, was Jack B., introduced a younger man to the audience.

The younger man stepped to the microphone and introduced himself as John (not his real name), an alcoholic. After the crowd responded back with "Hi John" he began to tell his story. In the first sentence, he told the entire crowd of 200 that just a few weeks earlier the Scottsdale Police Department had responded to his father's home and killed his brother. He was, of course, talking about me. In that very moment, I was convinced that Pat had taken me to this meeting and had set me up. I was convinced that it would only be a matter of seconds before the entire crowd of

200 would turn on me and kill me. As my heart raced, and my mind tried to keep up, I simply stood up, and began scanning the room to figure out who was going to come at me first, and how was I going to survive this.

Pat sensed what was going on inside my head. My heart was pounding, and I was scanning the room, fighting the urge to first beat the crap out of Pat, and second to go running from the place before they could get me. Pat grabbed me by the shoulders and looked directly into my eyes, and whispered to me that we were going to leave together. He told me that he would put his back on my back, and we would simply walk out. He told me that he meant me no harm, and only wanted me to get the fuck out of this place now. How he knew what I was thinking is amazing, because he said the exact words that worked. We walked calmly from that church into the parking lot where I was once again able to breathe. I nearly threw up, and I was emotionally drained. I went to that hopeless place again, just knowing that this is how I would need to live out my entire life.

Our exit was not unnoticed by Jack B; we met him later that evening at a breakfast diner and debriefed the incident. I am sure they had some laughs about it outside of my presence, but I was way too freaked out to think how ironic the situation was. I also learned something about Jack B. He was indeed former military, an Army Air Corps pilot who flew several bombing missions in World War II. More importantly, he spoke of how he and several others had experienced some recent success with helping others with legal problems by speaking to sentencing judges, and recommending 12 Step Meeting participation over incarceration. This, of course, piqued my interest, and I set about manipulating him to help me with the huge legal problem looming over me.

During the weeks and months that followed, I schemed ways to have Jack and the others rescue me from my plight. I met with them, attended 12 Step Meetings, drank coffee, and basically used these well-meaning people to further my own cause.

I read the Big Book, but only pages 83 and 84. The basic text of Alcoholics Anonymous (aka the Big Book) is a blueprint for living;

throughout this text there are examples of how to incorporate the steps into one's life. At that time in my life, I had no intention of doing the steps, but I wanted to reap the benefit. This was often the case in my life, although I did not become aware of this until much later.

On pages 83 and 84 of the Big Book there are what is known as The Promises, they are natural and logical consequences of having legitimately worked steps one through nine; it reads as follows:

If we are painstaking about this phase of our development we will be amazed before we are halfway through. We are going to know a new freedom and a new happiness. We will not regret the past or wish to shut the door on it. We will comprehend the word serenity and we will know peace. No matter how far down the scale we have gone, we will see how our experience can benefit others. That feeling of uselessness and self-pity will disappear. We will lose interest in selfish things and gain interest in our fellows. Self-seeking will slip away. Our whole attitude and outlook upon life will change. Fear of people and economic insecurity will leave us. We will intuitively know how to handle situations which used to baffle us. We will suddenly realize that God is doing for us what we could not do for ourselves.

Now these were and still are very attractive propositions, particularly to someone such as myself, who had been indicted, arrested, and was facing a long-term prison sentence. Not to mention the impact that my behavior had on my family, particularly my wife and soon-to-be first-born son. I desperately wanted those promises to come true for me, and I read them daily; I just wasn't willing to do the work to get them yet. Most importantly, I hadn't learned that nothing in this world, absolutely nothing worth having, comes without intention or initiative, commitment, perseverance, courage, faith, and some sort of spiritual growth. All these values add up to character, and at that time in my life, I wanted and desperately needed character; I just didn't have a clue as to how to obtain it.

So I read these promises daily, and sought to have others solve my legal and personal growth problems. God and the universe will not be fooled. Given my approach to problem solving, things did not go well for me, although, in retrospect, I have learned a great deal through these mistakes in judgment and execution. The criminal case against me gained steam as more and more witnesses came forward to testify against me. People who were once my friends would no longer associate with me, my wife Karen continued to be pregnant with our first child. But even though I had begun formal treatment for my substance dependence, my unwillingness to face my own deep-rooted defects of character would not allow me to stop drinking alcohol.

I experienced a relapse episode a week before I was to be in court. I attended a party that I had attended every year for close to seven years. It was a drinking party with close to 100 people in attendance. I resolved to drink no alcohol, yet attend the party. I arrived at approximately 8:00 pm; by 8:05, I was only going to have one beer; by 8:15, I was only going to have two beers, and so on.

By about midnight, I had drunk myself into an alcoholic stupor. In my addled state of mind, I reasoned that I would never be able to stay sober; if I continued to drink, I was going to die a lonely, tortured, agonizingly brutal, alcoholic death. Because this was not an attractive future, I decided to obtain a weapon, since I had surrendered mine, and take my life. I got a .45 semi-automatic pistol and went to the liquor store where I bought a fifth of whiskey. I drove out to the desert planning to drink the whiskey before blowing my brains out. I came to at sunrise with a broken bottle on the floor of my Jeep, and the loaded and cocked pistol in my right hand. I had gotten half the plan done...thank God I passed out and did not kill myself. That was the last time I drank alcohol; from that day to this, I have not had another drink, nor have I used any cocaine or mind altering substance!! The road to this point has not been rainbows and roses, but it has been sober!!!

Chapter 11

PUNISHMENT DAY

*I*n June 1986, I spent my days in the treatment center and my nights at 12-Step meetings, and basically was in sheer terror of what would befall me as the court date rocketed toward me. My lawyer arranged for a mitigation hearing, where we gathered family, friends, and professionals to speak on my behalf in an attempt to convince the judge not to send me to prison.

The police, probation department, and prosecutors all recommended a prison term. Our hope was that we could appeal to the judge's sense of fairness and convince him that I deserved probation rather than prison. I was focused on the upside of the plan: a positive outcome wherein I was granted probation with a small jail term. My attorney on the other hand, being more experienced in these situations and therefore more realistic, admonished me to "bring your toothbrush" to the hearing because I was likely going to prison.

I spent a lot of time with my mom during this period in my life. It was so difficult because she was just devastated at the prospect of her son having to go to prison. The guilt, shame, and anger at myself that I felt were exacerbated as I watched this woman give herself completely to the process of defending her only son. She was so angry at the police department for what she perceived as their part in my addiction, arrest, and likely imprisonment. She devoted a lot of energy toward defending me, even to the point of hiring a lawyer to look at the potential of bringing an action against the department. While she blamed the department, she also knew that I had a role in what was happening, but she focused on the department and how she believed they should have behaved. This is one of the cunning, baffling, and powerful aspects of addiction. Acting out of a thousand forms of fear she carried the fight throughout this ordeal, never wavering in allegiance to her son. It was difficult for me because I was in the process of learning that I was responsible for the choices I had made, and in her process she focused on everything but my choices. This is one way that addiction impacts families. One of the things that I will never forget her saying is that regardless of what I had done, I was her son. And nothing, absolutely nothing, could jeopardize her love for me. When she said that to me I was overcome with emotion and broke into tears. I sat at the counter in her home, she slipped her hand into her broken, adult son's hand and just held me as I came to terms with unconditional love from another human being. This is obviously a moment I shall never forget.

On the day that I was to be sentenced I woke up early and went to my attorney, Joe Chonekey's office to go over what was to happen and what to expect. I left my parents and my wife at the house and would meet them at the courthouse. Prior to leaving, as I got dressed, I found a note in my jacket. It was written by my mom and it read: "While you are standing there in front of that judge my hand is in your hand, love mom."

As I entered the courtroom on that Friday in late June 1986, I was with Pat and we both paused in between the sets of double doors into the actual court. In that small space we prayed: "God, I offer myself to you, to build with me and to do with me as thou wilt. Relieve me of the bondage of self that I may better do thy will. Take away my difficulties that victory over them might bear witness to those that I would help; of your love, your power and your way of life. May I do thy will always." It felt good to pray and yet scary to put my fate into the hands of a God who I had only recently made intimate contact with. We walked in and the hearing began.

Our side called our witnesses first. I can still see my mother up there on the stand testifying as to all my good qualities. What a courageous woman to go into that situation and to try her best to protect her son whom she loved despite his colossal wrong doings. As I picture her on the witness stand I am filled with gratitude for her willingness to go through with that, as well as with guilt and shame that my behavior led to her being in that difficult situation.

I had some friends who testified as to their knowledge of me and all the positive aspects of our lives together. My attorney had advised me that if we put my wife on the stand then the prosecution would counter with testimony from co-conspirators. As I scanned the courtroom, I saw one of the others who had been arrested but who had been given a walk for his testimony against me. I was so angry about the way this hearing went yet it had to be that way for me to learn the maximum from my mistakes.

The treatment professionals also testified as to the cunning, baffling, and powerful nature of addiction, and its impact on the community and people within that community. Of course, I focused on all the reasons as to why the judge should side with us and grant me probation for all my offenses. The professionals' testimony was for the purpose of convincing the judge to be lenient in any sentence he might impose. As I listened to their testimony, I was so much in denial about what was going to happen that I actually believed that their testimony was enough to sway the judge.

The prosecution put on witnesses that spoke of the nature of their relationship with me. I recall the matter-of-fact manner in which both prosecutors and police officers recommended jail time. The police also recommended that I be allowed to serve the time out-of-state for my safety. Years later, I would characterize this process as my side telling the judge all the good things they could think of about me, and the prosecution telling the truth!

After this process, I was given an opportunity to address the court. I told the judge how ashamed I was of my behavior, and how I would give anything to have the opportunity to make it right. I can recall standing there looking up at that man as he held my fate in his hands. In a very business-like manner, he sentenced me to seven years in the state penitentiary; then he pounded the gavel to signify the end of the hearing.

In that moment, despite knowing intuitively that I was going to get a prison sentence, I was just plain stunned. The very breath was taken from my lungs and my feet seemed to be rooted to the floor of that courtroom. I can recall looking out into the gallery where some people were crying and others were simply stunned as well, while still others were standing and looking for a way to exit that room.

I recall being directed toward the court officer who put handcuffs on me and began leading me from the courtroom. The tears came from me as I saw my wife and parents crying. The torrent of pent up guilt and shame just poured out. Once we got through the side door to the jail elevator I noticed that my attorney had been allowed to walk back there with me. The officer stopped me and both he and my attorney told me to stop and gather myself. The officer, God Bless Him, said "Hey look at it this way man, you will be out in three years; this could have gone much worse." My attorney didn't say much other than to express his sorrow that it didn't go as we wanted it to. The officer then told me that I needed to stop the tears because I was about to enter Maricopa County Jail, and I needed to be prepared for that reality.

I gathered myself, said good-bye to my attorney, and got into the jail elevator with the officer and began the descent from the courtroom to the Central Processing Section of the Maricopa County Jail System. Things were about to get real and different for me.

Chapter 12

I GO TO JAIL

*O*n a Friday afternoon in Phoenix, Arizona, the Maricopa County Jail is a busy place. There is constant noise. The first sounds I noticed were the metallic doors being opened with a distinct buzz and the sound of disengaging metal locking devices. That is a loud, constant, annoying, and almost brutal sound. This is most always followed by the grating of metal, until the thud announces that the portal is clear; the final piece of this aggravating cycle is when the metal door is then slammed shut to await its need to be opened again. Then the irritating rhythm is repeated.

While this is going on, prisoners are being transported to booking areas, holding cells, and other areas within the jail. There are also the loud voices of officers barking commands, prisoners talking back or making requests of officers, and the occasional sound of radio transmissions of communication between officers in remote areas of the jail. These sounds are acute to newcomers; yet to those who have been working in this environment; they are hardly noticeable.

The officer who escorted me from the courtroom that day removed his handcuffs from my hands and escorted me to a booking area. There another officer took custody of me. The first officer faced me and offered a handshake, wished me luck, and left the area.

The officer who had assumed custody of me had me empty my pockets. He cataloged all my belongings, and told me that they were very busy that day and he would get me booked later. He escorted me to a solitary holding cell that was clear Plexiglas on all sides. I was in that cell for nearly six hours and was then booked and assigned to a pod. Prior to being sent to the pod, my clothing was taken from me and I was given a jumpsuit. I was then escorted by two officers from the holding cell down a long tunnel to a room where they ordered me to strip out of the jumpsuit and stand in front of a machine that looked like a fan. This image is indelibly stamped in my consciousness: standing naked in the presence of these two officers as they deloused my body with chemicals. My humiliation, shame, and self-loathing had all reached new levels.

I was initially assigned to an open pod with approximately ten other prisoners. We each had individual cells that shared a common area; there were no windows, and I noticed immediately how blessedly quiet the place was. I was in total fear about my cell mates and, curiously, none of them said much to me upon my arrival, nor the next morning.

Early in the morning, two officers showed up and I was given the order to "roll up," a term which I learned meant that I was moving somewhere and I needed to gather my belongings. At this point, I had no belongings, so I just left the pod with the two officers. Once in the hallway, they stopped me and advised me that I was being moved to a segregation area for my own safety. They seemed to be sincere about their desire to protect me.

The segregation cell that I landed in was on a noisy floor at the end of a hallway. The door was solid steel with a trap used to insert food. My roommate was a large male who said very little upon my arrival or for the next several days that I inhabited that place.

At night, the officers placed a television out in the hallway and we were able to watch an hour or so of television. I can recall the irony of watching the Baseball All Star game on July 4, 1986, in a jail cell, through a slot in a metal door. Life had certainly changed for me, and in the recesses of my mind I knew that the choices I had made had a lot to do with those changes. I was not a happy camper!!

One afternoon, an officer appeared at the doorway and entered the cell. He told me that I would be leaving the next day for the Arizona State Prison Complex. That's all he said, and then he left. I went to bed that night knowing that another change was coming, yet I didn't have any idea about what that meant. I was about to learn. At approximately 5:00 am that morning, a couple of officers showed up and gave me the order to "roll up." After collecting my meager belongings, I was placed in handcuffs, body and leg chains, and moved downstairs to a single-person holding cell. Several others who were being transferred were stationed in a larger cell awaiting our transport. Things were going to get real and different again, I just knew it.

not to show it, and they both knew it; I later learned that they had been through this same dance on their first arrival.

I was ushered to a rectangular chain link cage, which ran along the east wall of the large processing room. The cuffs were removed; I was placed inside the cage and told to sit on the bench. I complied, and the gate/door at the end of the cage was padlocked closed.

The prisoners who had been waiting outside were then brought inside; all were cuffed together on a chain. With their possessions, they were gathered into the center of this large room; soon the corrections officers were barking orders to this group of men. The cuffs were eventually removed, and the processing began. Each man was stripped, fingerprinted, photographed, and his property was inventoried. At the end of this process, an orange jumpsuit was issued, and each man was then escorted from the room to another place.

As I watched all this unfold, I said nothing; I simply sat and watched. Suddenly, a large, tattooed Hispanic man squared himself on the cage I was in. "Fucking pig, you're dead meat man; over on Dog Ward, you're mine." This was met with cat calls from everyone left in the room; they all stared at me, looking for the fear, looking for some weakness to exploit. The pure ferocity of this situation was palpable. All I could do was look back at him. I said something like "Bring it," which led to more cat calls, laughter, and knowing looks of menace, malice, and intimidation. At that point, I took a gamble and called out to the nearest correctional service officer. "Could you put him in here with me?" I asked loud enough for all of them to hear. I had the most menacing scowl I could muster on my face as I made the request/statement. The three that I pointed at all disappeared into the crowd of inmates and the entire room went silent for what seemed like an hour.

The moment was interrupted by the entry into the room of a man in a corrections officer uniform; he wore a bronze oak-leaf on each collar. He was impressive; his command presence was apparent to everyone in the room. Major Al Bauer was in charge, and everyone in that room knew it.

He walked straight over to the door of my cage. He looked at the nearest corrections officer and said, "Open this up." The man complied. The major looked at me and simply said, "Come on," and motioned with his eyes toward the open room. I really wasn't sure I wanted to go out there, but looking at the major, I thought that I didn't want to be in conflict with him either.

I walked out into the room and walked with him toward a door on the north side of the room. He opened the door, and motioned me into the office. I walked in, he followed, and closed the door. He motioned toward the single chair on the other side of the desk. I sat down. The contrast between the pandemonium in the processing room and the quiet stillness of an office was tangible. My eyes never left the major. He looked at me, and in a New York accent said, "I'm Al Bauer, I'm the chief of security here," as he extended his hand across the desk to shake mine. I hesitated then shook his hand. He then reached into his uniform shirt pocket, drew out a pack of Benson and Hedges menthol cigarettes, and threw them on the desk in front of me. "Go ahead and smoke one," he said.

Again, I hesitated; accepting anything from anyone, especially corrections personnel, had some implied meaning; it could be interpreted as me being a snitch, or now owing something to the giver; in all cases there was risk associated with even the smallest act. "I said smoke!" I took the pack as soon as he said the words. He lit the smoke for me, looked directly at me, and said, "You're not going to die here." My ears burned, I exhaled the smoke. How did he know I was thinking that? "You are going to make it out of here," the unmistakable New York accent just added to my already reeling senses. "I brought you in here to talk with you. I read about your case; they hung your ass out to dry boy. There's no way they didn't know what was going on with you; and when they saw a way to dump you and get away, they took it." He spoke the words so quickly, and with such conviction. I kept staring at him waiting for him to say something, anything about me that was evil, or bad, but nothing came. He just looked at me, not with pity, or even commiseration, he just flat believed what he had said, and didn't care what anyone else thought. "So look here now; you are to hit first and ask questions later. If anything, and I mean anything, happens, you tell my corrections officers that Major Bauer, the chief of security for the Phoenix Region, has given you permission to do whatever you need to do to survive. I mean it. You have better training, and more experience with people, than most of the folks working here; there's just no sense in you dying here."

I couldn't believe my ears. Here was the chief of security for the Phoenix Region telling me to tell the corrections officers that he had given me permission to do anything I deemed necessary to survive. I was absolutely blown away...also, I had no idea what to expect from this place.

"You're gonna learn a lot of things here; the most important is that you are not a bad guy. I have lots of experience with bad people, and you aren't one of them." The words hung in the air. I didn't know it then, but I had been waiting for someone, anyone who wasn't part of my family, my treatment group, or my defense lawyer to say that to me. Years later, Jess Medrano, the man assigned to be my parole officer would say the same thing, and I had the same feeling then... but in the immediate situation, I had to survive.

"You're gonna go back in that room there, and no one is gonna hurt you; now they'll say some things, try to intimidate you, but you can't let it get to you, or show them the fear. Look at me, you go back in there, look 'em in the eye, and know that you are gonna make it through this." He said the words with such absolute conviction that I actually believed him for a few seconds. I still had some fear, but I felt better knowing that he believed I was gonna make it through this.

"Let's go!" Back into the processing room we went. This time, he took me to the middle of the room, moved a couple people out of the way, and told a corrections officer to get me done. He then left the room.

The officer's name was Abril; he located the box of my belongings, told me to strip, and began processing me in. Now being naked in front of several other men in a prison is a demeaning, humiliating situation to begin with; I believe my sense of awareness was heightened because of the fact that those I was with knew that I had been a police officer, and literally all eyes were on me, or at least it sure felt that way.

After the search, I was given my underwear, and an orange jumpsuit, and ordered by Officer Abril to get dressed. We then inventoried all of my belongings, which weren't much, and then I was photographed, fingerprinted, and asked some medical questions. At the end of this process, which took about a half an hour, Officer Abril looked at me and asked "Do you want to be in Protective Custody?" At this point in time, the entire room became quiet, so quiet you almost hear the ticking of the clock on the wall. Everyone was waiting to see how I would answer this question.

I had been advised about this situation. Protective Custody or "PC" is an administrative classification designed to protect individuals who have known issues with members of the general prison population. Those in protective custody are segregated from others, housed in special cells, and basically live a miserable existence amid those who are living a "normal" prison life. Typically, those in PC are given one hour per day outside their cells, when corrections personnel are available; it is truly "hard time." Moreover, once an individual is stigmatized with the PC brand, there is no chance for trust or coexistence with members of the general population. Often during prison disturbances, attempts are made to get to those in PC to kill them. The protective custody population generally consists of people who have testified against others, child molesters, law enforcement personnel, or others who require segregation from the general population for other reasons. My attorney had advised me not to request this status under any circumstances.

So here I was, being asked if I wanted to "PC up." I could see the others in the room looking intently, waiting to see which way I would go. I looked at Abril, and hoping that my voice wouldn't crack, I said, "No." What seemed like an eternity passed; in actuality, only a few seconds elapsed before the room erupted.

"Woo Hoo!!! Gonna be a good time on Dog Ward tonight! Here we go, gonna have some fun now! The Man gonna be learnin' stuff now!

They were all laughing and carrying on while I waited for Abril to tell me where to move to. All he did was point toward a closed door and grin. His face said "You are in deep, deep shit fella, and I can't wait to see how this goes." His voice said, "Go through that door, you're assigned to Dog Ward." I went through the door.

Once out of Processing, I was escorted to an "L" shaped pod with four-man cells on each side of the hall. As I was walking down the hall, there were cat calls, threats, and all manner of yelling. The officer with me ushered me to an empty cell, closed the metal door with the chicken wired window, and left me inside. I was instantly relieved; I felt safe, secure, and, at the same time afraid, of everything. I had no control over anything. What would happen next? Who would come to the door? Who would they put in the cell with me?

As these thoughts raced through my mind, I could hear the others around me yelling their threats; after pacing inside the small cell, I laid down on the metal bunk, with a view of the door, and waited for whatever would happen next.

While lying on the bunk, my head spinning, in total fear, shame, and dejection, trying to simply make it from one moment to the next without completely losing my mind, the door suddenly opened and an officer appeared with another prisoner.

We both looked each other over. He was a kid, no more than 20-25 years old; he gave me a knowing look. I think we both recognized the fear in the other. He stood about six feet tall, with a stocky build; he had none of the tattoos that so many of the others had. He just stood outside the door looking in at me, as I stood rooted in the center of the cell looking out at him.

The officer motioned for him to enter, and he did. We exchanged a silent greeting, eyes to eyes, and a nod of the head only. I sat on the bottom bunk, while he went to the sink and got a drink. The door closed, and we were alone in this small cell. My mind was moving at a thousand miles an hour. What do I say? What do I do? What are the rules? No situation I had ever been in prepared me for this moment.

Thankfully, the door was suddenly thrust open again; an officer summoned me out, and told me I was to go see my counselor. Wonderful, I thought. As I stepped out into the hall again, I saw a prisoner buffing the floor with one of those big buffing machines; I noted that his eyes never left me as I walked by. The catcalls started from the cells again as I walked by. When would this end?

I was ushered into a room where I met with a man in civilian clothes, who I was told was a counselor. As I was introduced by the officer, I extended my hand to shake hands; this guy looked at me and said, "Never shake hands with any staff member. First off, they won't want to have physical contact with you, and you will learn that shaking hands with us will not look good to the other inmates." I quickly retracted my hand. He said, "Dude, you've got a lot to learn, and a short time to learn it."

After he directed me to sit, he asked "How ya doing?" What a question. I mean I just want to rewind this whole deal. I'm barely making it from one moment to the next, and this guy wants to know how I'm doing. I told him I was doing as well as could be expected under the circumstances, although I really wished I could be some other place. He told me that they were working on classifying me. That is an assessment of my violence potential and escape risk. He told me that it didn't help matters that I had killed a guy not long ago, and that I was a former law enforcement officer. He said that his job was to determine which institution I would be sent to, to do the time I had been sentenced to. He did say that I was eligible for "good time," which equated roughly to being eligible for release for good behavior at about one half the original sentence. I told him that I was really interested in that aspect of the situation; he chuckled, and told me that everyone is interested in that. He said that the time for me would be hard; there would be constant attempts on my life, and that I would have to be constantly vigilant to survive. He spoke of the options about where I would do my time. He quickly assured me that no matter where I went, I would be a target, death threats would be the norm, and I was dealing with folks who could very easily, without conscience, kill me. While this information was unsettling, I had figured that out in the short time I had been at Alhambra.

He told me that my best option was to stay at Alhambra as a resident worker, and he would be checking that option out for me. After our conversation, I thanked him, without shaking his hand, and was dismissed from his office. The officer returned and I asked about making a phone call; he checked with the counselor, who authorized the call. I was taken to a pay phone, one that only allows for collect calls. This phone was on the wall in the middle of the corridor where the cells were located, not a real private location at all. I picked up the phone, and called home to my mother.

In this phone call, it was so difficult for me to hold back the tears; I was so ashamed, and dejected. Throughout the call I kept it upbeat, assured her that I was completely safe, and would likely be housed in the Phoenix area; this was important to her because she wanted the ability to visit me. The call lasted for about 10 minutes, and I hung up hoping that I could keep up the charade.

As I was lead back to my cell, the cat calls returned: "Gonna fuck you up! You're dead meat motherfucker!" I ignored it, and walked back to my cell. Internally, I was thinking about how I could stop that, and how much it just pissed me off.

When I got back to the cell, the officer opened the door, and I was confronted with a new situation; now there were four other people in the cell, and this scared the crap out of me. As people were through in the processing room, they were now housed in the cells on Dog Ward; I had five roommates, all of whom had observed me enter the system. Now my mind snapped back from the shame, guilt, and anger, to how to manage the fear, and stay alive in this new living arrangement.

As I entered the room all eyes were on me. They had been playing cards, seated on the floor in the middle of the cell. I went to the sink to get a drink, and the door closed. I'm stalling for time trying to figure out how to handle this. I finished the drink, as they resumed the card game. This was good; they weren't looking at me anymore. I looked at the bottom bunk where I had first laid down;

the kid who had been in there when I left looked at me and said "I told 'em that was yours." I said "thanks" and lay down on the bunk and pretended to be interested in the card game. The same kid says "if you wanna play next you can."

Again, my mind is working a thousand miles a minute: Well at least they haven't attacked me; they seem interested in the card game (I will learn later that anything to break the monotony of doing time is good.); or is this some ploy to get me to drop my guard so they can kill me. And what did it mean that the others seemed more interested in the card game than the spectacle of what occurred about an hour earlier in the processing room. They had to have seen. Why are they not saying anything about it? But come to think of it, I'm glad they aren't saying anything. Trying to figure out how to read every other person's response, and how to negotiate each and every breath, was just excruciating. This whole deal was gonna take a lot of getting used to.

For some reason there was no more dialogue; they played cards, and I lay on the bunk and stared at the walls, or the door. The door soon opened, and it was time to go to chow. We all filed out, formed a line, and left the building. Once outside, I saw huge, red brick walls that formed a quadrangle. On the tops of these walls, officers patrolled looking down upon the prisoners as we lined up to go into the chow hall.

There was chatter and banter, and I sensed some relief on the part of the others to be out of those cells. For me, I was all about observing what was going on around me. I kept thinking as the line disappeared into the chow hall: Are there metal forks, and knives? How are we seated? Where can I go to reduce my risk of being killed? Who is behind me, and how do I defend myself? All these things were on my mind as I made my way into the chow hall.

Once inside I was instantly relieved to note that the utensils were plastic. Well now at least that was one good thing. The room itself was expansive, yet as a group we were filling it up fast. I would be forced to sit with three other prisoners at a four top table. I got my food, and looked for a place to sit. I chose a spot that had three others already sitting there. Once I sat down, one of those already seated gave a sarcastic sneering laugh, looked at the man on my right, and said "Oh great, now we're fucked; you know what's comin' next." The cat calls started again. I just ignored it all, looked at my food, and ate. After a few moments (that seemed like a lifetime), the noise abated, and those around me resumed eating their food.

At this point all I could think of is: "What happens when I am done eating?" Where do I go? What happens then? This is a microcosm of what each moment was like.

When I finished eating, I got up and followed the others to a corner of the room to return the tray and utensils; I had to walk through a room full of people who stopped and glared at me as I passed them. The pressure was intense, and dealing with it was becoming more difficult, although it did not seem like I had much choice.

Outside the chow hall, we were all directed back to Dog Ward, and into our cells. As I was let back in, there were two others there, both had been there before so there was some relief; not long after the cell door closed, a prisoner walked by, looked into the window slot, flashed a gang sign, laughed, and said "You sorry motherfucker, how do like it now?" He then left the window slot and continued down the corridor, presumably to his cell.

The two guys in the cell with me both looked at me for a response. I said nothing; the moment was awkward as they waited for me to say something. One of the guys, the younger one, said "It must be tough for you...I heard you were once a cop." I said, "Nope, that's a rumor, those guys just need someone to be pissed off at." It was the first time we had spoken. They exchanged glances back and forth from themselves to me. While we tried to figure out what to do next, the cell door opened and the other two guys were let back in. It was quickly decided that we should play cards, and we were then able to avoid having to talk much more.

The rest of that afternoon was spent playing cards and just making small talk. Later an officer appeared at the door and told us we could go take a shower if we wanted to. The shower room was down the corridor from our cell, and there was a prisoner standing outside that door handing out towels. As the five of us left the cell and headed for the shower, I noted that there were several other prisoners inside the room showering; the majority of those in the room at the time were Hispanic. Once they observed me, the conversation changed; I understood Spanish (thank God) and was able to hear them plotting to choke me with the towels once I was inside the shower. I turned back, found the officer who had escorted us to the shower room, and suggested to him that it might be better if I were allowed to shower last. He gave me a knowing look, nodded, and agreed to this suggestion. I went back to my cell and waited until everyone had showered and was able to go last. What an absolute miracle that I stayed alive that long.

I slept fitfully that night; so much was going through my mind. I was too afraid to sleep for long; I reacted to every noise. People walked in the corridor, and officers often came to the door to peer in the small window. I was so angry with myself for making the choices to use drugs; I was also angry with the prosecutors, the judge, the investigators who brought the case against me, and with Ronny who had sold me out to keep himself out of prison. Admittedly, most of my anger was misdirected to others; I was still having difficulty accepting that I had played a major part in all this.

On the morning of the second day in Alhambra Prison, after breakfast, I was summoned from my cell and taken to meet with Captain McClleand, the facility chief of security. He was a slightly built man, who wore glasses and appeared very scattered to me. He made no pretense about sizing me up, and after that launched into diatribe about what he expected of me if I were to remain at Alhambra.

I learned later that the counselor had made the recommendation that I stay at Alhambra because security and control of prisoners was better there. As a result of this recommendation, the various layers of supervisors were notified, and apparently had decided that this would be an acceptable reality. The interchange with the captain was part of my interview process to see if I would measure up. None of this was conveyed to me, and I was to learn later that this was business as usual for this organization.

After about a half hour, we left the office and he told me that we were going to meet Martha, the woman who would supervise me as a resident worker. We left the room on Dog Ward, and I followed him out onto the yard and across to a room that served as an occupational therapy area for prisoners.

Once inside, I was introduced to Martha, a tall, white haired woman, whose kind face, soft soothing voice, and gentle demeanor belied the place we were in. She looked like everyone's Grandma. Martha shook my hand; she had a strong grip. She looked me straight in the eyes as she asked if I wanted a drink of water before offering me a seat in her office.

The captain left the room and waited outside the small office where I was seated across from Martha's neat desk. She asked if I would be comfortable working with other inmates. I hesitated, and she offered that the inmates that I would be working with were either mentally ill or low functioning. I couldn't imagine what this meant, so I told her that I could do it. She told me that she would help, as would her assistant, Terry, and she would appreciate having someone on board who she could depend upon to help with her group.

I was unaware at the time, but this was a very special relationship. In the world of the prison, there is a definite pecking order, with the prisoners/inmates at the bottom of the list. Relationships are defined by mission. There are the Security Group, Programs, Administrative, and prisoners/inmates. For this woman to tell me that she wanted to depend upon me for help was really uncommon, although I was completely oblivious to it at the time. I just was unaware of the dynamics of this place, so I simply said I would do as she asked. She told me that she would take me on a tour of the place and as we emerged from her office she spoke to the captain: "Hal and I will be making a tour of this place, if you want you can go back to your office, and I'll call when we're done." In this case, the use of my first name was significant; it meant I was a person, not just a number or chattel to be used to complete a task; this is the way Martha lived, even in the world that was this prison. What a shining example of how to treat people; I am forever grateful for her living lessons. The captain agreed, and left.

We walked and talked as she showed me around the Occupational Therapy room. It was one of the first times that I actually felt able to breathe, and my heart was not racing. I was protected by a locked door; there were actually windows that allowed me to see out onto Van Buren Street. I saw cars going by, people walking on the sidewalk, but what I remember most is the sunshine coming into the room casting shadows, and the light on the burnt orange floor of the room. This was definitely a stark contrast to the cell I had spent the last day in.

As we talked, Martha told me that I would be working with prisoners who participated in occupational therapy each day. I would be helping her and her assistant, Terry, in supervising these prisoners, and cleaning up the room after them.

I would learn several things about this later. First, the prisoners she talked about were severely mentally ill people who had committed some of the most bizarre, and often violent crimes. Second, the assignment itself was most unusual because Martha and Terry would actually be depending upon me to assist with this most interesting group of people.

Martha told me that I would be granted access to the Occupational Therapy room on the weekends, and I would be able to participate in projects she had the others doing. This whole situation was a wonderful opportunity; and at the end of our time together, I was absolutely ecstatic.

She called for the captain to return, and in a few moments he reappeared and Martha and I said our goodbyes. She informed the captain that she thought I would work out as her assigned resident worker.

The captain and I stepped out of the door to the Occupational Therapy room, and onto the prison yard. I noted immediately that the yard was occupied by an entire ward of prisoners; I'm guessing 50-100. All were wearing orange jumpsuits, and were basically moving around the yard talking, smoking, playing volleyball, or just sitting in the shade. Every sense in my body was instantly alerted. The transition from the earlier conversation with Martha to tactical considerations was instantaneous, and very necessary if I was going to stay alive.

I followed the captain as we took approximately ten short steps to a door next to a large smoked glass window, which I would later learn was dubbed "The Security Office." The captain opened the door, turned to face me, and said "I have some business here, you go ahead over to Dog Ward, press the intercom button, and ask them to let you back in; I will call them to let them know you will be leaving there today." He said this with that sick twisted smile on his face.

Dog Ward was located on the other side of the prison yard, fully one hundred yards away from where I was standing. To get there, I would have to cross through the yard, and the 50-100 prisoners that were in that yard. This was the first time I would be outside, in the presence of those who had threatened me previously, and the prospect of making this walk across the yard was daunting to say the least.

The captain ducked inside the room, and closed the door. I was on the yard, all alone, and I had to do something quick, as I deduced that standing with my feet rooted to the sidewalk was not real promising.

I turned and began walking across the field toward Dog Ward. I passed several of the prisoners, most of whom simply ignored me. I felt somewhat confident out in the middle of this yard/field, but as I closed the distance toward Dog Ward, the spacing began to shrink, and I recognized how potentially dangerous this would be.

At about 25 yards from the door, I heard the voice: "Oooh you're all alone now asshole." I looked directly in the direction of the voice, and kept walking toward it. I observed a man in an orange jumpsuit, 6' tall, dark skinned, anglo, a menacing smirk on his face; he was walking directly toward me. "Yeah dude, I'm alone, but so are you, come and get some." Where these words came from I have no earthly idea. I squared myself onto him, and strode purposefully toward him, my arms akimbo, eyes dialed right into his. This guy was by himself, and immediately stopped in his tracks. I could see, and even feel the fear in him. It was truly astonishing. I closed the distance between us, never breaking stride, or the look into his eyes.

As I got within five yards of him, he actually stepped to one side, and dropped his gaze to the ground. He was beaten. I was in that game-time mixture of fear and adrenaline, and how I kept from slugging this guy I have no idea. I strode right past him, and closed the rest of the distance to Dog Ward, all the time praying that this guy would not turn and come after me. He didn't.

Upon reflection, this event had to happen. It would not be the last challenge; however, it had to occur to set the tone for how I was to survive. I can't call it living, because I was in a constant condition yellow, which is no way to live. But this event shaped other events to come, and helped me to understand some of the dynamics of prison life.

I made it to the door to Dog Ward and I pushed the intercom button. Without having to say anything, the electronically operated door clacked open. I entered, began breathing again, and prepared for the next challenge, whatever that might be.

Chapter 14

DOG WARD

The first weekend in prison I spent on Dog Ward. I was locked in a two-man cell with several other guys. I had spun the ruse amongst my cellmates that the others were mistaken about me being a former police officer. I told them that I was, in fact, an Air Force Officer, stationed at Luke Air Force Base, who had been convicted of numerous DUI's.

While I am sure they all had their doubts about my story, for the time being nobody challenged it. The weekend consisted of playing endless card games, reading the Bible, sleeping, and making three trips per day to the chow hall to eat.

The time passed ever so slowly. My emotional state was erratic. I vacillated from self-loathing to intense anger toward Robert, the informer; Scottsdale P.D; the prosecutors, the judge, and the criminal justice system in general. I felt incredibly ashamed of my behavior, and at the same time angry at myself for being so weak and stupid. Nighttime was the worst. I lay awake thinking about every stupid thing I ever did, how I had wasted a career, and the shame I brought to my family. I felt so powerless to help Karen, who was pregnant with our first child. I spent endless hours thinking about how hopeless the future looked. Fortunately, the circumstance of being in a place where I had to be tactically prepared to stay alive afforded me some relief from the thoughts of what a first class idiot I had been.

So many thoughts swirled through my head that first weekend. I was so preoccupied with self-loathing, and how ineffectual I was for Karen, although it was in those moments that I resolved to do whatever it took to stop doing drugs and avoid bringing any shame to myself or my family ever again.

When Monday came, I was summoned from the cell, and taken over to the processing unit. There I was given some of my personal items, a pair of blue jeans, a blue chambray shirt, and a pair of work boots. I traded in my orange jumpsuit for these clothes, and I was also issued a mattress, sheets, blankets, and a pillow. I carried these out of the processing unit, and followed the officer as we made our way to Baker Ward.

As we walked through the prison yard toward Baker Ward, I had no idea what to expect. I was just really happy to be out of the jumpsuit and headed toward new surroundings.

As we entered the interlock leading into Baker Ward, I wondered what was waiting on the other side of the door. Nothing I thought of prepared me for what lay ahead. As the door opened, the first thing I saw was an oversized leather chair that was bolted to the floor. The chair had restraint straps attached to it, and it just looked ominous.

Several prisoners were walking freely in and out of cells that had opened doors. All were dressed in blue jeans, prison type tennis shoes, and gray sweatshirts. None looked healthy, physically, and it seemed like they were all smoking.

The ward itself was an L shaped affair with cells on the outsides of the hallways; in the middle was a glass and chicken wired booth occupied by officers. This was the housing area for seriously mentally ill prisoners. Along with the officers assigned to this unit, there were several correctional service counselors, who worked to keep these prisoners contained and secure.

As I traversed down the first section of the ward, taking all this in, my eyes were drawn to the control booth. Inside the booth were several officers, and at least one correctional service counselor. I recognized the counselor immediately; His name was Mac; we had both played on the Department of Public Safety football team for the previous two years. As our eyes met, he smiled warmly (not menacingly or smugly), and rolled his eyes upward as if to say this is one hell of a place to meet again. As I continued down the corridor, coming out of a room that I would later learn was the counselor's office, I recognized Randy, another man I had played football with. When he saw me, he was visibly shaken. He nodded silently and hurried past me toward the control booth.

The next situation I encountered was truly amazing to me. In the end corner of the corridor I was walking in, I observed J.B., a kid whom I had arrested at least twice. He was actively hallucinating, talking out loud to someone/something up on the ceiling in the corner of the hallway. He was talking non-stop, and briefly glanced at us as we walked down the hallway. What struck me was the fact that as this guy was hallucinating life continued on around him as though he was not even there.

The officer and I arrived at a door and he instructed me to drop my bedding. When I did, he handed me a key and told me that I was to unlock the door, go inside, and locate a bed. Once I had done that, I was to report to the control booth, as I was required to meet with Baker Ward Staff to review the rules about interaction between resident workers and Baker Ward prisoners. He told me also that I was to be sure to secure the doorway into the workers' quarters because as Baker Ward residents were not allowed in there. I went into the room and found that it was empty of people. There were several bunks and wooden lockers arranged in corners of the room; it was dark and quiet. I found an empty bunk, the one closest to the door, so I made the bed. Because I had no personal belongings, save those I had on my back, I had no need for the locker. As I sat on the bed, all alone inside this room, I was able to see out onto the yard through the gun port- type windows. The yard was busy with prisoners milling about. I was inside, alone...safe for this moment, yet between two worlds--on the outside, prisoners waiting to be classified and moved to their destinations; on the other side, seriously mentally ill prisoners who had little idea of reality. Where did I fit in this equation? How did I get into this mess? How do I survive? When do I get out of this deal? All of these questions and more confronted me as I contemplated my situation.

I snapped out of this period of reflection, and went out into the hallway and down to the control booth. As I neared the booth, both Randy and Mac signaled me to a wait there. They emerged from the booth and escorted me back to the counselor's room where they said we would wait for the lead correctional service counselor. Once in the room, with the door closed, both acknowledged our prior relationship; they shook hands with me and told me how horrified they were to read about all that had happened. They both expressed how sorry they were that the situation had turned out the way it did, and pledged to do their best to see that I survived this ordeal. I was so thankful for their presence, and their support. In the stark brutality of that prison, with all the harshness and evil present, the slightest kindness is magnified and intensified. I was truly blessed to have those guys present in my life at that time, especially with their frame of mind. We had played football together for two years, and the bond forged through facing opponents on those fields stood for something in our relationship. They did not judge me for what weakness I may have displayed; they simply remembered how we had faced opponents together, and they stood ready to offer their assistance when one of their own had fallen. This is a rare quality among people, and was greatly appreciated by me.

Soon we were joined by the senior counselor; he greeted me cordially and asked if I knew what Baker Ward was about. I told that I did not, and he explained basically that it was two separate worlds. The majority of the unit consisted of seriously mentally ill prisoners who all had special needs. There were frequent "takedowns" when prisoners acted out. Most were long timers, and the majority committed crimes against persons ranging from armed robberies and aggravated assaults to murder. The officers and counselors were there to maintain order and basically keep them from killing one another. Interaction between this population and the resident workers, though inevitable, was discouraged.

The resident workers, a population of approximately 10 prisoners, had access to their quarters, and the remainder of the Baker Ward Residents did not. This was strictly enforced. Also, resident workers had access to matches and lighters and the Baker Ward residents did not; they were relegated to using the wall mounted heat sources for lighting cigarettes.

This process took about 10 minutes. The senior counselor then asked if I had any questions; I told him no, and I was dismissed. I went back to the room, let myself in, lay down on the bed, and just thought about my situation. I was alone, starting to get hungry; I was alive, facing the better part of seven more years in this place. I wanted to cry; however, I knew better than to do that. So I just laid there and eventually drifted off to a fitful nap.

I was awakened by the sound of voices. There were now several others in the room, and I didn't know any of them. They all stayed on their side of the room, and while there were several glances, no one said anything to me. They talked amongst themselves, and soon drifted out of the room to places unknown to me; I was left to my own thoughts about my current situation.

Soon some more prisoners drifted in. This time, one of them came to my area and said "hi." He told me his name was Mike, and that he had heard about me from the guys in processing; this guy was way overly friendly, and I knew instantly that there was some kind of game going on here. He offered to show me around, and to answer any questions I might have. This guy was my own personal welcoming committee--how nice. Later, I discovered that the man was blatantly homosexual and was attempting to groom, or cultivate me to be sexually active with him. Once I was on to him, I made it known that I was not interested. He did admit at a later time that he was targeting me.

As other people began returning from their day's work, I was introduced to them all; about 10 in all, we all lived in the same large room, which was sectioned off to accommodate us all. As a group, we left our room to report for count, a practice that we had to do several times daily; after this it was off to the chow hall for dinner. I was starting to feel good about being part of this group; there was something empowering about belonging that I was attracted to. But this feeling was short lived, for I was soon again confronted with a hostile environment.

I had to enter the chow hall, get a tray of food, exit the building, and sit at a table with the others to eat. It sounds pretty simple except for the fact that I knew none of these people, and this chow hall had one door in and out. It was also a place where I had been initially confronted, and I didn't feel good about going in there. Compounding all of this was the fact that once in and out with the food, the groups from both Dog and Easy wards would be coming to eat and that posed an entirely new threat.

As I went in and got my food, I surveyed my options. First off, I hung back and let everyone else go in first, giving me the ability to at least watch what was happening in front of me; it also gave me options for when I came out to sit and eat. A simple thing like where to sit was actually a complicated issue in a prison environment. Seating patterns had already been established long before I arrived, and a mistake here could be dangerous, even fatal. Being last was a good choice because it allowed the others to maintain their rituals, and allowed me some choice in how to protect myself. I quickly devised the following plan: the tables were situated just outside the entrance/ exit door; if I were fortunate enough to get a seat facing that door, I would be able to see those entering and exiting and my back would be to the prison yard. This plan posed a problem until I realized that the windows of the chow hall would provide me with the ability to monitor what was happening behind me. As I reflect upon this now, I can recognize how this seemingly mundane situation was fraught with subtleties that, in my case, needed to be addressed for me to survive the moment. As it turned out, I was able to secure a position on the corner of a table, allowing me to see the chow hall, and use the window to monitor my back. I sat at that same table, in that same spot, for each meal for nearly three and one half years.

After we ate, we all returned to Baker Ward. That's when the games started. My first contact with anyone was with a tall, blonde kid named Jamie. Now Jamie approached me as I lay on my bunk. He walked over from his area and leaned onto my storage locker. As he looked down upon me he said that he had been in processing and had seen me come in. We talked briefly about what a horror show that was. He seemed pretty easy to talk to, which immediately alerted me to the fact that something here was not right. That intuitive sense was right on. Jamie soon began to manipulate the conversation toward sex. He informed me that there was no "straight" sex in this place, and the only hope of any sex at all would be with another man. Now, I had heard all the stories about prison, and sex, and I was more than a little bit annoyed by this come-on, so I let him know that I was not at all interested in any more talk about sex, or sex at all. I remember how he looked directly at me, sneered and matter-of-factly stated "That will change." I would later learn that Jamie was openly gay, and was the lover of a large man who had been convicted of murder, and had, at one time, been involved in a prison gang, but had snitched someone off so he was now being protected at Alhambra. I would also learn that this relationship was known to staffers, and was actually enabled by the captain of the security force at Alhambra Prison.

While I had been talking to Jamie, I managed to learn where the laundry was, and was able to get my clothes washed. After he had left and gone back to his area with his bunkmate/lover, some of the other guys came over to introduce themselves and find out about their new roommate. One of those who didn't come over was a Hispanic man who seemed very leery of me, and as a matter of fact everyone else. I learned later that this guy was alleged to have been in the Mexican Mafia, or EME, and had testified against them, and was in quasi-protective custody. In fact, there were times when he would actually be placed in an isolation cell on Dog or Easy Wards for days at a time.

As evening approached, I was overtaken with an extreme sense of loneliness, alienation, and sadness. It was just so damned quiet in this large room. There were people, but they kept to themselves, speaking to each other in hushed tones. Hanging in the air was a sense of resignation, loss, and hopelessness. It was powerful and horrible at the same time. I silently cried myself to sleep that night, and I remember thinking how utterly hopeless my life was, and was always going to be.

Upon awakening the first morning off of Dog Ward, I was filled with remorse and guilt about my circumstance. This was to be a common theme every day, with work being a welcome respite from my own mind. So I was now ready to take on a new role in life--I was a resident worker at Alhambra Prison.

The first order of business was to be counted. I was required to report to the central control area, press a button, and wait for acknowledgement from an unseen officer on the other side of the window. This ritual was repeated twice daily. After counting, it was off to breakfast.

Once inside the chow hall, I got my tray of breakfast, and proceeded outside to the picnic tables; there were several prisoners already there as I moved to my chosen spot. As I sat down, the man next to me said "I didn't say you could sit there, now did I."

In that moment, I knew I was about to learn something. I was instantly alerted to the fact that all eyes were on me, and this had the potential of being a defining moment. I stood, looked at him, and acknowledged that he had not granted permission for me to sit there. He looked back at me and asked me if I wanted to sit there; I told him I did, and he told me that it was ok. This apparently was some kind of test to see how I would respond; the prisoner, I would later learn, was an Arian Brotherhood member, who was rumored to have been an enforcer for that group. There would be a series of tests like this. In fact, for the first year of life in this prison, I would be learning the culture, rules, and norms of this society.

In a moment, the tension subsided; people went back to eating their breakfast and talking amongst themselves. I actually wanted to interact, but did not dare because I was not yet part of the group. I had the feeling that I was tolerated at best.

After finishing breakfast, I headed off to the Occupational Therapy building across the yard, and to my first day at work. I arrived at the building and knocked on the door. I was greeted by Terry, Martha's assistant; he was a very soft spoken man, and was always very respectful to anyone I saw him interact with. He greeted me, let me in the room, and immediately told me that he had secured a set of keys for me that would allow me to come to the occupational therapy room at will. Now the implication of this set of circumstances is huge. Essentially, I would be allowed to come to this place and not have to be with the other prisoners. At that moment, I knew this was a bonus, but I was not yet aware of how great a blessing this actually was.

Soon the first group of prisoners arrived for their occupational therapy time. It was a group from Baker Ward. This is where the criminally insane prisoners were housed. Those who weren't actively hallucinating, or acting out, were given time for occupational therapy. Basically, these guys came to work on all manner of crafts such as making leather wallets or belts, woodworking projects, macramé, and cups/pottery fired in a kiln. The kiln was kept in a room next to the main occupational therapy room, and I would be required to take the projects over to the kiln, fire them, and bring them back to be painted and finished. I was to learn that these were major responsibilities, and the prisoners depended upon me to care for their projects. Basically, their projects became their lives; these objects were the only things they had, and in this lonely, austere existence, a wallet, belt, cup, or macramé plant holder were some folks' only hold on sanity.

Another aspect of my job was checking out tools to the guys. Now the tools, like razor knives, hack saws, awls, and other implements were kept in a room on a shadow board. My job was to hand out the tools as they were requested; and at the end of the time period, I was to collect them back, and Terry or Martha would check the shadow board to ascertain that none left the building and found their way back to the wards. It wasn't long before I saw the irony in the fact that I was virtually handing weapons out to some of the sickest, most dangerously insane people in the prison. I was amazed that no one ever acted out, and while there was an occasional argument, or shouting match, nobody was ever injured physically. I believe this was the work of Martha and Terry. Their combination of people skills and desire to help others was enough to manage this tough population.

I came to cherish my work in the Occupational Therapy Unit; I had a key to this room, and was able to access this place essentially whenever I wanted to. This was especially nice since privacy in a prison is a rare commodity. I was able to come to this place after a days' work, just to collect my thoughts, and, if nothing else, to be away from the threat of being hurt or killed by others. Additionally, on weekends, when time really dragged, I was able to come to The Unit, and write letters, listen to Arizona State University Football games, read, and perhaps gain some perspective on my situation.

Martha and Terry encouraged me to utilize the facility to learn things like macramé and pottery projects. I actually took advantage of this, and made several macramé plant holders for my family members, as well as pottery projects. As I look back, it was good for me to take my mind off the futility of my situation, and the revulsion of my behaviors that brought me to this place.

During the first few weeks of being in prison, I had struggled for about two days with depression until another prisoner confronted me about it. He had to have been one of God's angels. He was a black man whose name escapes me now, but he was an old time convict who had seen some things in his time and decided to share some insight with me.

I had been assigned to the resident worker crew and in that first week so much stuff happened that I was overwhelmed simply with the adjustment to my new prison lifestyle; my thoughts were still mired in what I had done to earn this position. I kept replaying all the events, trying as best I could to alter the outcome. Time after time I engaged in this wasteful behavior with the same result. It led to an extreme sense of pitiful, incomprehensible, demoralization accompanied by a sense of self-loathing that is nearly indescribable.

I hated myself, my life, my God... everything. I would rail at God daily about my anger with him for allowing this to happen to me. I questioned the wisdom of my being born. I was totally consumed with anger, regret, remorse, and shame. The only interruption from these thoughts were moments of tension when I had to think about how to stay alive. This combination of my horrible self-image, and the prison environment, replete with living examples of the worst behavioral examples that society had to offer--me included--led to me being sad (an understatement), dejected, hopeless, and generally miserable.

This apparently caught the eye of my benefactor, the "Old Timer" who very simply confronted me outside our living quarters one day. He had no elaborate speech or elegant mannerisms. In a simple, straightforward manner he said: "Look here sonny...you in a bad, bad way; you gotta stop this here down in the dumps stuff or it gonna go bad for ya." I asked him what he meant and he responded: "Sonny boy the past is the past; you jes gotta let it be." How did he know? Who told him what I was thinking? "This a whole new game now and you gotta get through this to get over to the other side; having the blues don' do ya no good up in here." He turned and raised his arm toward the prison yard and even then his eyes were alive with promise and he had a genuine smile on his face and in his voice. "This yo place now...this where you gonna live and you gonna make a life here. You gotta start right now believin' that you can get up outta here, but for now use what you find here." I was astounded. How did he know this is what I needed to hear? How did he have so much faith? Why did he think to share this with me? I started to ask him these questions but he cut me off. "You don' need to ask me no questions; you don' need no mo from me. You jes gotta do the deal sonny. Now get on with it; and if you don't, you gonna be dead soon." And he sauntered away, leaving me with my questions unanswered and my mind spinning a million miles an hour.

As I lay in my bunk that night my mind was still working on what the old man had said. I started to believe, just a little bit, that I could actually make something happen that would benefit me. This certainly wasn't the most conducive environment for learning, or was it? I started developing a plan to deal with the next seven years. I knew that I had the most hope of success if I stayed sober, and to do that I had to learn the concepts from those who were living that kind of life. Not too many of them were here in this place, but I had the Big Book of Alcoholics Anonymous, so I resolved to read some from that every day. I also decided that I was going to begin believing that Whoever created me was benevolent and had me in this situation to learn something...perhaps something that I could pass on to others. Maybe, just maybe, I could take my experience in this horrible place and put it to good use for myself and others. If I was mired in a morass of self-pity and destructive self-deprecation then I would have little hope of successfully doing anything. In short, I had to change my attitude. Now this is a very simple concept but rarely easy. For me, it was complicated by the fact that I had a fairly high opinion of myself to begin with; however, a quick survey of my surroundings left me with the thought "This isn't what I had in mind." In this way, I made a humble beginning. I was able to empty my mind of some preconceived notions that actually served to hold me back and I began what has become a lifelong journey of learning to make lemonade from lemons. I think, given the environment I found myself in, I intuitively realized that there was so much negativity, so many traps to catch me, that I had to become adept at walling off the nay-sayers, blocking out those who would doubt themselves and their own abilities and felt an overwhelming need to project that onto me and others. Perhaps the most difficult aspect was to push the internal fear aside and trust that I could somehow make a go of it, even if I couldn't see where this was going to lead.

So I resolved to live each day, each excruciatingly painful day in this place to the best of my ability. I chose to see the struggle as a pathway to peace, and to be the best person I was capable of being, and to make the best of the lessons afforded me.

Chapter 15

MY SON IS BORN

espite my attempts at changing my attitude, I was still afraid, angry, resentful, and I "knew" that this whole recovery thing was not going to work. Almost immediately I was greeted by the prison chaplain, a very kind, tolerant, and patient man named John, who came around every week and invited me to the Tuesday night 12-Step meeting on Dog Ward. Each time he came by, he stopped and chatted with me and I politely refused each invitation. I was so angry that I had gone to treatment, gone to 12-Step Meetings, read the book, and even prayed now and then, and got sent to prison anyway! That became everyone else's fault so I saw no point in attending 12-Step Meetings anymore. This is akin to taking some poison with the intent of another person dying! God bless John because he kept coming around, and coming around, so that I relented and went to my first meeting in prison just to get him to quit bugging me.

I will never forget that first meeting on a Tuesday evening on Dog Ward. Two men came in from the outside and ran the meeting. One was Bob, a large, barrel chested, wild man who was so brash about telling his story that I was instantly drawn to him. He wound up coaching/sponsoring our softball team. The other man, Bill A., was a short, bespectacled attorney who I eventually worked with years later. Bill A. was a former prosecutor who had been sober awhile and was carrying the message by chairing weekly meetings at Alhambra prison. This energetic man was full of enthusiasm for living a sober life. His energy and his commitment to being sober and carrying the message to others were inescapable. His initial message is indelibly stamped into my consciousness and even today I can recall that first encounter with particular fondness, although, as is so very often the case with me, fondness wasn't my first reaction.

The meeting was held on Dog Ward, and I was very anxious because I had to go over to there and was locked in a day-room with approximately 30 or so men in orange jumpsuits who were awaiting transfer to other prisons in the state. I was wearing blue jeans and a state-issued blue chambray shirt, with my state-issued brogans. Prison 12-Step meetings are interesting, to say the least. I learned later that the majority of the people at these meetings are there simply to get out of their cells for a while and to drink the coffee that was provided for the meeting. This is not to say that some folks are not there to bring about change in their lives, but the majority appeared to be attending for other reasons. Bill A. started the meeting with a prayer, and a couple of prisoners volunteered to read the preamble and other meeting materials. Bill A. then told his story, and it was during the telling of his story that he said something that I hope I will never forget as long as I live.

As he neared the end of his remarks, he pointed his bony little finger directly at me and said: "If you like what you've been getting, just keep doing what you've been doing." I was instantly incensed. It was all I could do to keep from getting up and kicking his scrawny little ass right there in the day room on Dog Ward. I was so angry that I almost didn't hear what he said next. "But if you want a different result, or change in your life, the 12 steps will bring that change about." All I could hear reverberating through my head was the "If you like what you've been getting" part. I was filled with self-righteous indignation. Here I was sitting in a state prison and this guy is talking about if I liked what I was getting. It was literally all I could do to keep from planting this guy! We still share a laugh about that even today. It was a key part of my eventual recovery.

Now I would really love to tell you that I instantly incorporated the steps into my daily living and changed the course of my entire life. That didn't happen. I stayed really pissed for about a week or so. I replayed my whole life and stayed stuck in the idea that it just wasn't fair that I was in prison, publicly shamed, humiliated beyond imagination, and now people wanted me to admit to being an alcoholic and change my approach to living through the 12 steps. I was so full of pride, arrogance, and self-delusion that I couldn't even begin to conceive that this should, or even how this could happen.

So after a week or so of living in a new resentment, something happened that I still can't explain. I attribute what occurred to the Grace of a kind, faithful, loving God. I woke up one morning and decided that I would give this crazy idea a chance. I happened to be walking across the prison yard and the thought came to me "Normal drinkers don't wind up here." I literally stopped in my tracks right in the middle of the yard. I looked around me, even up to the sky, perhaps seeking some sign from God, but none came. I stood there and thought about that thought. I had never heard those words before; I had never thought that thought before. I was genuinely perplexed. Then the calm came--a sense of comfort that I had not experienced before. I stood in that spot for several minutes and then I started laughing, mostly at myself. This moment started me on a new way of looking at my life, specifically a new way of looking at my relationship with alcohol and drugs. I actually began to believe that maybe, just maybe, this approach of learning the 12 steps, and the way recovering alcoholics approached life, would have some benefit for me. Maybe I wouldn't have to live the rest of my life in prison, or the prison I had created within myself trying to be someone I wasn't.

I continued attending that 12-Step meeting on Dog Ward every Tuesday night. I met some very nice people who came into the prison and shared their lives with all of us. I started reading the Big Book, and I began the process of reprogramming my mind about my relationship with alcohol and drugs.

Within a short period of time, I witnessed an incident that has been permanently stamped in my mind. I think of this occurrence daily, even today. I had occasion to traverse the prison yard for some reason in those early days, and had become adept at choosing the safest times and methods for accomplishing this task. On this particular day, I left the Occupational Therapy Office and headed north across the yard, noting that there were several prisoners from Dog or Easy Ward in the yard. I skirted the crowd but my attention was drawn to three men who were in the middle of the yard laughing, high fiving each other, and basically having a good old time right in the middle of a prison yard. I was struck with their brazen joy and celebratory nature. Something in me guided me closer to them, and even though it was counterintuitive to my safety and well-being, I could not resist getting closer to them to find out what they were so very happy about. As I got closer to them, I could hear them talking and in a few short moments I discerned that this group of three were a grandfather, a son, and a grandson. Yes, three generations of one family!! And they were celebrating the fact that all three had come together in the prison yard. I was stunned. Nearly rooted to the ground as I watched this sad reality unfold in front of me! I watched these men laughing and joking about their being in the same prison and I was nearly sick to my stomach. My wife was pregnant with our first child, and the message could not have been any clearer to me!! Change your thinking and behaving or this is what is waiting for you and your family!! I moved on from them as they continued their dance and I was forever changed. Thank You God!!

In the ensuing days, I found solace in religious literature. I was really afraid of God so I trod lightly in this area. I did find some comfort in reading tracts and listening to preachers on tape. I started going to AA meetings and at one meeting I got a bookmark that advertised an AA tape library. I called the number one day and learned that it wasn't really a library; they actually sold AA speaker tapes. When I explained to the man that I was in prison and was unable to pay for the tapes, he took my address and promised to send me tapes. He told me I could pay him by "passing it on." The tapes arrived about a week later; I listened to several speakers, one of whom I met years later on the outside. I was able to share with him how much he inspired me as I lay in a prison bunk listening to tapes at night.

So each day became an adventure, and I would love to report that everything was rainbows and roses but that's not the truth. Life in that prison was hard. I was lonely, afraid, sometimes bored, yet I became good at seeing the positives in seemingly hopeless situations.

I continued attending that 12-Step meeting on Dog Ward every Tuesday night. I met some very nice people who came into the prison and shared their lives with all of us. I started reading the Big Book, and I began the process of reprogramming my mind about my relationship with alcohol and drugs.

One day, I was walking across the Alhambra prison yard and I saw that two men wearing civilian clothes came through the main entrance and were walking across the yard toward me. There was no obvious threat as they strode toward me and I toward them. As we approached, they both greeted me in a friendly, non-threatening manner. So easy going were they that I dropped my guard for a moment and for some odd reason, after acknowledging them, I inquired as to where they were going.

This turned out to be a life changing event. They told me that they were going to a 12-Step meeting over on Dog Ward. I had no idea that there was a day time meeting on Dog Ward. They invited me to accompany them, but I knew that I would have to get permission, so I told them that I would check it out with security and, if approved, would join them.

I went to the Security Office and after several minutes of explanation and seeking permission from all the Powers That Be, I was granted permission to attend the meeting. Once I got over to Dog Ward and then inside the day room where the meeting was, I sat right next to one of the men who had come to facilitate the meeting. He was a soft spoken, silver haired gentleman whose words both infuriated and intrigued me. He spoke of a peace that passed all understanding, and the ability to go where other free men go without having to struggle or fight with anything or anybody. He also spoke of a group of people on the outside who weren't judgmental of us being here; they were supportive and wanted us to succeed at staying sober and having a decent life.

I didn't believe a word he said, yet deep down inside of me I wanted to believe every word he said. What a monumental conflict of thoughts and emotions. I hatched a plan. I had been told by Bill A. that I needed a sponsor so an idiot would not be running my life; now I had an idea of what he was implying, but I kept my mouth shut. I also knew that having Bill A. as my sponsor would not work. But this other guy, his name was Bill S., had, in his soft-spoken way, pierced both my soul and spirit with the truth of his words; it was a great lesson for me. I also harbored a secret desire to prove him wrong about all that stuff he was saying about people wanting to help a guy like me. I just knew that couldn't be true. After all, who would want to help a convicted felon and former cop who had killed someone and disgraced the badge and uniform.

So after this first meeting I asked Bill S. if he would be my sponsor, and he agreed. This was the start of a relationship that would lead to my being released from prison, living a life free from the bondage of alcohol and drugs, going to college, and eventually marrying my wife Ellen and having a family. None of these things did I ever believe I was capable of attaining, and each of these things Bill knew I could have. Amazing stuff, but it did not happen overnight. Like any relationship, we had to have a beginning, and ours was forged by weekly contacts in prison 12-Step meetings. Moreover, he and I actually created a Friday night 12-Step meeting at which we were the only two attendees for several months. During that time, he and I were able to process my journey through the steps of the program.

Our relationship was not without some conflict. In our first meeting, I felt it necessary to expound about how much I knew about life and being sober. I mean, after all, I had several months without any alcohol or drugs. Bill listened with bemused patience and to this day I will never, ever forget his reaction to my attempt to impress him with my vast knowledge. He looked at me and in a very matter-of-fact tone said, "You know with most people I start them off at step one of the program, but since you are who you are, I've got a special idea for you." Now in my mind as he said this I'm thinking "Finally someone is capable of recognizing true talent." He continued: "Because of where you are in this deal I'm not gonna start you at step one; yours is a special case, so your starting point is different than most anyone I've ever worked with." Again my mind was really working overtime about how unique I was and how fortunate I was to find this wonderful man who was obviously very intelligent. Bill then said: "Before you get to step one your job is to simply quit being an asshole."

The breath just sucked right out of me. For one the few times in my life I was utterly speechless. You could hear the ticking of the clock it was so quiet in that visiting room. Bill simply looked at me waiting for me to react to his message. My mind was working furiously to take in what had just occurred. I was ready to pound him into the floor, yet that still small voice inside me told me to just do nothing.

For several minutes the silence just hung there. I knew he was right, but making the admission was gonna be difficult for me. With as much humility as I could muster I simply said, "OK, how?"

Bill taught me how to pray to God. Not the kind of prayers where I asked him to do stuff for me, but a humble request for me to recognize moments where I might be of service to someone else. This was obviously a radical departure from any kind of mindset that I had been able to assume for quite some time. The process of addiction to alcohol and cocaine had created such a persona in me that I had become completely self-serving and everyone was able to see this but me. This man had studied to be a priest and was one of the most spiritually aware people I've had the good fortune to know. He was precisely what I needed to begin the process of recovering from the hopeless condition of addiction.

We worked vigorously on the steps of the program. We met weekly and I actually began the process of changing. One of the most poignant moments came when I did my 5th step; which is admitting to God, to ourselves, and to another human being the exact nature of our wrongs. Bill was insistent that I write this out just like it says in the Big Book; the challenge was my being in prison where all my possessions were subject to search at any time by the prison staff. Some aspects of my situation weren't known to law enforcement and the specter of writing this stuff down scared me to death.

Prayer, faith, and a degree of willingness to do whatever it took to be free from the bondage of alcohol, drugs, and my own preconceived notions about life motivated me to write out the details of my past misdeeds. On a Friday night in the fall of 1986, I sat with Bill in the chapel of Alhambra Prison and shared with him these dark, ugly details of a riotous life run on self-will. In the days leading up to this event, I was anxious, restless, irritable, uneasy, and generally not good company for myself or others. On that evening, the emotions in me ran high and as I relived these moments in speaking them to this stranger who had befriended me I felt worthless, empty, hollow, and spiritually bankrupt.

This process changed not only my view of myself, but my view of humanity. At once I began to see that my life so far had been an exercise in attempting to wrest all I could from everyone I came in contact with. Sure there were moments when I contributed to a given situation, but for the most part I nearly always had an angle that I was working to gain something for myself. Faced with this realization, I was filled with guilt, shame, remorse, and a sense of self-loathing that turned into fear that I would be rejected by not only Bill, but all who knew any part of me. As I read from the papers I had written, he listened intently and now and then nodded his head. He spoke little but I knew intuitively that he was keyed into what I was saying, and perhaps more importantly what I was experiencing on an emotional and spiritual level.

After what seemed like hours I came to the end of my identification and confession of the exact nature of my misbehaviors. I looked expectantly to him for some sign of reprehension, revulsion, and rejection. None came. He looked at me with soulful eyes and simply asked, "Is that all?" I thought for a few seconds, and then added some stuff about my behavior since being incarcerated; again he asked if that was all. I told him that it was and he immediately suggested that we pray. I don't remember what we prayed but I do remember feeling good about praying to a God who could somehow be in this place with us as I faced a lifetime of hurts, habits, and ineffective living.

A healing tranquility was coming over me and I had no idea where it came from or how to respond to it. I simply began to cry as I felt the release of a flood of dammed up emotions that had not been expressed in years. This very private moment with a man I barely knew is indelibly stamped on my consciousness. After I regained some semblance of composure, he told me that I was to be commended for my effort of honest self-appraisal. This started a whole new flood of tears and some laughter from him. He noted that for some kind of tough convict type I sure had sweaty eyes.

Before Bill left for home that night, we agreed that while this beginning was good, it was simply a beginning. He was often fond of saying that while "faith without works was dead, so was work without faith." So, in that context, we set out to work the remaining steps of the program. The last thing that he told me before he left that night was that he believed that I had passed by that "special starting point" he had recommended weeks before. We had a good laugh at that and I went back to my bunk, read from the Big Book, and fell asleep knowing that change was happening in my life.

One day, I was at the small prison library looking for a book of some kind when I happened upon an algebra textbook. Now on the surface this doesn't seem like a big deal, but actually it was. I had never been any good at math, having received no grade higher than a D in high school math classes. So here I am in the Arizona State Prison living this hopeful, positive, glass half full very likely fantasy existence when up pops this algebra book. I quickly dismissed it from my mind and tried as best I could to ignore its presence by moving away from that rack. Now my mind is talking to me: Why are you moving away from that algebra book? What are you afraid of? The chatter would not stop no matter how far away I got. I found myself now with the book in my hands reasoning that all I had was time, so maybe I could take this book and learn some algebra. So I took the book back to my cell and actually began to read the introduction. I learned that this book actually had the answers to the even numbered problems in the back, so I ever so tentatively began working from the first chapter of this stupid algebra book. Well I am proud to say that I worked through that entire book and as I write this I have a huge smile on my face because it reminds me that I am capable of doing anything if I put my mind to it--even algebra.

For the first two months as a resident worker, I was allowed contact visitation on the weekends. My mom came to visit every weekend. I was of course overcome with shame, guilt, and remorse at having her come down to a prison to visit her son. She was so loyal to me and by her example I learned what commitment and family really meant. A memorable visit came when the administration allowed us to visit outside the walls at a picnic table in the shade of a huge Mulberry tree. The sensation of the wind on my face, hearing cars going by on the street, and a Tupperware container with French toast, butter, and syrup were small things, but recognizing the value of those things and how much they meant, and still mean to me, is something that I hope I never forget.

Those visits continued nearly every week for the entire time I was in prison. The guilt dissipated some as I realized that this woman was spending her energy giving to another as was her true nature. She taught me so much about unconditional acceptance of another human being. This may have been one of the single most important lessons that I had to learn, yet it was not easy. Prison had a way of keeping me focused on all my bad behaviors and how I had disappointed this wonderful lady who did not deserve this difficulty in her life. It was during those Sunday visits that she and I would talk about how life would be once I left that horrible place. Her inspiration and motivation were instrumental in my surviving prison, and my having a can-do attitude once released.

When I was sentenced to seven years in prison, my wife was three months pregnant with our first child. I was so afraid for her; I felt so ashamed that I would be in prison when my wife gave birth to our child, unable to contribute to the welfare of either one. My guilt and shame were palpable and constant. I talked with my wife almost daily, and wrote letters. Her family and especially my mother were so very supportive of Karen in those dark days. I have no idea how she managed as well as she did; certainly it had nothing to do with me because I was languishing in prison.

My son, Kevin, was born on a Sunday; December 28th, 1986. I know it sounds weird, but I knew something was happening that day. On Sundays, I usually watched football games on television; I was totally unable to concentrate that day. I learned of his birth the next day, and was absolutely ecstatic. Major Bauer was too; I remember him talking to me about the importance of being a good father to my boy. I wondered then how it would be possible for me after being in prison.

Karen brought Kevin to see me the next visitation day. What an absolute joy to see this baby boy. It was also deeply shameful to me to realize that the first time I saw my new son--he was four days old—was in the visitation room at Alhambra State Penitentiary.

One of the more notable aspects of that day was my first diaper change. Kevin was totally uncooperative; in fact, he peed on my shirt, all the way up to the shoulder. I was ecstatic!! My wife was absolutely mortified. After she left, I showed everybody the wet spot. I am sure they all thought I was completely nuts!!

There have been several bright spots in my life throughout the years. This day of seeing my firstborn will be etched upon my memory forever. And I have to say that God has been so gracious to me. Some of my deepest fears were about missing milestones in my son's life. I have to say that God has been so great in allowing this boy, now a grown man, to have a relationship with me. We have spent countless holidays together, gone on hunting and fishing trips, gone shooting together, gone out to dinner with his girlfriend, and a thousand other things that my God has allowed us to share during my life here on earth. I am so grateful for this relationship!

The time I spent at Alhambra led to my learning several lessons, none of them were easy to learn, but some were especially painful. One in particular was the time that I asked another resident worker for a cigarette and he agreed to give me one. I also needed a light so without asking, I picked up his lighter and was in the process of lighting the cigarette when he hit me square on the jaw. He continued by raining down blows on my head and shoulders, and just to make the lesson complete, ended with a few well-placed kicks to my side and back. In all, this lesson took approximately 30 seconds. As I gathered myself and eventually got to my feet, he pointed at me and gave me a commentary about the proper respect one should have for others.

Another situation occurred when I was assigned to maintain the visitation area. This required that I wash and wax the floors, empty the trash, and clean the restrooms in the visitation room. Sounds simple, but it wasn't. This area is where visitation occurs and thus where contraband is left by those visiting. The contraband itself and the myriad of ways to leave it are only bound by the imagination of those involved. In this case, someone had left something that I was supposed to find and deliver to one of the resident workers. The only information that I got was that something was in that room and if I found it, I was to bring it to a specific person. The best part about this whole situation was that I was particularly ignorant; I had only been told that I would find "something." But try as I might, I was unable to find whatever it was that I was supposed to find. This turned out to be great for me because a snitch was also at play in this drama, and the second I emerged from the visitation room I was stopped by the on-duty lieutenant and searched. The officer found nothing on my person or in the trash I was emptying. All of this occurred while I was being observed by the other prisoners/resident workers. I gave up nothing under questioning, which was a good thing for others to see, and I eventually was left to go about my business.

The next day, a Monday, when Captain McLelland returned, I was summoned to the security office. The captain ordered me to sit while telling me that he was not happy with me and all the tension I was causing. Of course, I was incredulous and countered with my take on the whole situation, which was some sort of conflict between two others that I got put in the middle of it. The good captain would have none of it and ordered me to "roll up" because I was being placed in segregation for my own good. My initial reaction was pure anger. I was totally powerless over this situation and did not like it one little bit. Self-pity soon followed as I was placed in a segregation cell, and for what I didn't know.

It's sometimes difficult to picture prison as a place where spiritual growth occurs but it does happen and this was one of those times for me. In that segregation cell, all alone, I had a chance to look at me and how my behavior had a great deal to do with my situation. That segregation cell was a dark place with no glass mirrors, only a stainless steel plate over the sink/toilet apparatus. But in that place I realized that I had run out of people to blame for my situation. There was no snitch, no police, no prosecutors, no judge, nobody but my reflection looking back from that makeshift mirror. And I saw, for perhaps the first time, that I was accountable and responsible for my choices and the consequences that resulted. While this realization was revealing, it was also hard to abide, yet a very necessary aspect of my eventual recovery process. I spent several days there and eventually was released and, within days, transferred to Flamenco Prison.

Chapter 16

MADHOUSE OF A PRISON

After approximately one year in Alhambra Prison, Warden Stan Bates paid me a visit. He told me that there had been some security issues and he had made the decision to transfer me from Alhambra to Flamenco. I knew nothing about Flamenco and because of the security issue I actually welcomed the change. Though he didn't say it, there had been some tension among the resident workers and, for whatever reason, shifting people around appeared to be the simplest method of smoothing things out.

Flamenco Prison is a high security unit that houses some of the most dangerous men on the planet. Many are certifiably mentally ill, most are heavily medicated, and all are highly unpredictable. When the pressure of prison life and mental illness comes together and spills over into the lives of others the result is often violent.

Along with the mentally unstable prisoners in this place were two other distinct prisoner profiles. First was a group of prisoners that had been found to be HIV positive. This group was housed in a secured wing and consisted of approximately 20 individuals. This group was separated from others by a metal chain link gate that divided the wing into two distinct sections. At certain times, the gate was opened and these individuals were allowed access to the small, cramped chow hall and to an exercise yard that was secured with 10-foot high fences, and a full complement of razor ribbon.

Movement for this group was often restricted, and, in general, the wing that housed this group was small, poorly lit, and depressing--a ghastly place.

The other distinct group was the resident workers. This group consisted primarily of folks who were in some form of protection. I was in this group, and we numbered approximately 10-15 depending on situational factors.

We were housed on the chow hall side of the fence separating the tier from the HIV group. There were cells on either side of the tier, and directly across from my pod was a shower facility. There were six of us in the pod. The pod had a toilet that was basically in the middle of the room and afforded no privacy whatever. My cell mates were often transients moving from one prison to another, although there were some who lasted a while before being transferred.

Once I settled into Flamenco I went through a major adjustment. First off, the physical plant was much tighter. My room was occupied by seven others, and ours was the second cell in a long, narrow wing of cells. Ours and the one next to it were separated from all the others by a chain link gate. All those living on the other side of the gate were HIV positive, and therefore segregated from the general population.

Going away from the chain link fence was a small hallway that emptied into the chow hall where all the prisoners in Flamenco ate their meals. Wings on the other side of the chow hall held the criminally insane prisoners. Inmate-on-inmate fights were daily occurrences, as were "take downs" orchestrated by the correctional service officers assigned to supervise this diverse, mentally unstable, and dangerous group.

Essentially, I was in the midst of two highly dangerous groups-- the HIV prisoners and the mentally insane. The HIV group consisted of some career criminal types, some young first timers, and some tweeners; most were depressed and fatalistic in their approach to life/death. Some just didn't care. In a mean, sullen way, they showed by their body language and behaviors that they should be given a wide berth, lest one become a target of their malevolent, malicious, and vile anger at their condition.

The criminally insane, who comprised the majority of prisoners at Flamenco, were unpredictable, unstable, heavily medicated, and highly erratic; these guys could go off in seconds. I now recognize that the stress level at this place was incredible for all concerned--prisoners, corrections officers, medical personnel, and administrators. In an environment that was so unpredictable, the only predictability was the constant florid displays of mental illness--men talking to imaginary others, rigid body postures, drooling, take downs, four pointing, and strapping people to chairs. These situations took their toll on everyone associated with that environment.

There was a third group. Several of us were in need of placement outside the general population due to social situations that were unique to each person. Some were snitches, some were gay, some were law enforcement/corrections, and some were suspected organized crime figures who were in some form of cooperation with the government. This group of 10-12 was literally sandwiched into quarters that were between the HIV crew and "The Nuts." It was a stressful, demanding, and nerve racking existence and it is where I lived for approximately one year.

One man who made an impression on me was the son of a parole officer. "String Bean," as he was called, was six foot four, and as thin as a rail. He was very intelligent, and was prone to expounding on philosophical themes that were often above my ability to comprehend. He was a friendly, jovial sort who favored smoking marijuana and this had led to a number of legal entanglements and his eventual imprisonment. I actually met his father during a visitation by my mother. In a private moment, the parole officer asked me to befriend and protect his son. In that brief moment, I came to a glimpse of understanding the powerlessness, helplessness, and fear experienced by loved ones of those incarcerated. In that same moment, I got a small piece of realization as to what my own loved ones were experiencing. In that brief moment, when a man reached out to me to help his son, I gained some understanding about the impact of my behavior upon others, and I was thrust back into guilt, shame, and remorse for having done the things I did. I recall looking the parole officer in the eye and telling him that I would do what I could; the relief in his eyes was palpable even though we both knew that prison life was bigger than both String Bean and me. String Bean left our unit, and I read in the newspaper that he had died in his sleep while in the prison he was transferred to. I hope that was really the case.

One of the most amazing things I learned in that year was the myths about mental illness. Up until this time, my experience with mental illness had been limited to isolated instances of people acting strangely and the law enforcement response of maintaining order and protecting people from themselves. In this prison, there was every form of mental illness one could imagine. Psychotic behavior manifested by auditory and visual hallucinations, delusional thinking, bi-polar mood disorders, and simple issues like depression and anxiety.

During afternoons, I would find my way out to the exercise yard where the mentally ill guys would be walking, smoking, or maybe even lifting weights or playing basketball. This is where I met Karl, a soft-spoken man about six foot three with a slight build. He was quite insane, being treated for paranoid schizophrenia. He walked and smoked constantly, and engaged in constant chatter to no one in particular. His fingers were stained an orange color from the nonstop smoking of hand rolled cigarettes. I would run around the exercise yard and he would walk and smoke. We saw each other every day for nearly a month before I recognized that he would look for me and would follow me around. This relationship was forged in that institutional kind of way that can only be understood by those who have been in such a place. I was not aware of the relationship at all until the day I brought a chessboard out to the yard.

Now this was no ordinary chess board. I had saved some money and purchased a chess computer made by then champion Gary Kasparov. I had sought permission from the administration to have this chess board and was denied, but I had the thing sent to me anyway. Once I got it, I began playing chess daily as a way to relieve stress and occupy my time. On the day that I brought the chess board out to the yard, Karl spotted it instantly. As I explained earlier, he and I saw each other daily, but had not spoken a word to one another. As soon as he saw that chess board our relationship changed. He came directly over to me and told me his name. Then he asked if I would play chess with him. We sat at a table and broke out the pieces while he shivered with anticipation and I believe he smoked two cigarettes just in that process.

It's important to remember that this is a man who is heavily medicated, and rarely speaks to live people, but speaks constantly to those he imagines are present. Once we got the board set up, it became obvious that I was overmatched. This guy was so skilled at playing chess that I don't believe I ever put him in "check" for the several months that we played. I am certain that I never won a game! I can say that Karl and I had several deep conversations and I learned that he was a person, not simply a diagnosis or a problem. He was a living, breathing human being who was so very intelligent, yet there were misconnections in his mind that led him into trouble. We played every day for several months until he was transferred to another prison, and I never saw him again. Thank you Karl for teaching me about personhood!

In this madhouse of a prison unit the security detail was led by Captain Lutz, a sturdily built red-haired woman who had a quiet, businesslike presence. I had two memorable contacts with her. I had initially been assigned to work in the kitchen as a food server. This meant that I was one of several prisoners working a line putting food on individual trays, including the trays of the security officers.

For some reason that I can't recall, I accidentally touched the food of the security sergeant with an ungloved hand. The dude went completely off. He was a short, blond haired, high strung, Napoleon-like man. He began screaming at me from the chow hall floor through the window of the serving line. His public tirade lasted for several minutes in front of the prisoners eating their dinner. I apologized several times and prepared another tray. This only served to escalate his anger as he yelled even more and ordered me out from the kitchen to the security office adjacent to the chow hall. I complied with his order and was met at the door by a contingent of security officers who escorted me from the chow hall entry door to the security office. They actually pushed me into a chair in front of the sergeant's desk. The door was closed and I found myself in the room with three security officers and this enraged sergeant. Perhaps out of ignorance or denial I wasn't afraid; I sat there and listened to the sergeant berate me for a good 5-10 minutes. His reactions were clearly over the top so I just listened as he kept on and on. Now perhaps I should have been more afraid, but for some reason I wasn't. After all, I had been living with fear for the past couple of years, a former police officer in prison surrounded by people who didn't understand me and hated me just for existing. I guess this guy going off just didn't really impress me a whole lot. When he finished, I looked at him and asked "Are you done?" Well this was good for another several minutes of yelling and screaming, all of it obvious to those in the chow hall eating. In a strange way, this behavior by the sergeant actually helped give me some credibility with my fellow prisoners. After the tirade ended, I apologized for making the mistake of touching his food and shut my mouth. He thrust some papers in front of me and ordered me to sign them. It was a disciplinary write up and I complied. I was then ordered back to the kitchen to resume work with the food crew. Once I got back and the security officers were out of sight, my teammates came to me and expressed their compassion over my public castigation by the sergeant. This whole ordeal was a very strange occurrence. I was taken aback by the sheer ferocity of his anger and didn't know what was going to happen with respect to the write up.

The next day Captain Lutz summoned me to her office. She closed the door and asked me to describe what had happened. I got the impression that she was more concerned about the reaction of her staff member than my mistake touching the food. I told her my version of what had occurred. Then she did something that I thought was very strange; she asked me what I thought was going on with the sergeant. I told her that I thought he must have some problems that he was dealing with because his reaction to me was way over the top. Without saying anything, she tore up the write up, told me to steer clear of that sergeant for the day, and said she and the overnight sergeant would be meeting with me that night to discuss a reassignment.

My mind immediately went into high gear trying to figure out what all this meant. It turned out to be a good thing for me. I met with the captain and the overnight sergeant that night. Also present were a number of the overnight security officers. This meeting consisted of these officers letting me know that they knew of my overall situation and, while not necessarily sympathetic, they were obviously empathetic, which I was grateful for. I didn't know it then, but I was actually interviewing for the job of overnight cook. I would report to work at 10:00 pm in the kitchen and would be responsible for preparing the food for all the overnight correctional staff, and the overnight prisoner work crew. At the end of this confab, I was offered the job and I accepted it. The benefits were huge. I was basically working an opposite schedule from the majority of the others, thus minimizing contact with other prisoners. But perhaps the most important issue in this whole scenario was the fact that some people emphatically stated that they trusted me. Looking back, this turn of events was another stage in my recovery process.

The games that go on in prison are varied, sometimes complex, and ever-present. The correctional service officers assigned to any prison have the job of recognizing, deciphering, and responding to a never-ending torrent of manipulative and divisive behaviors. One of the guys assigned to the kitchen detail, and one of the maintenance crew, were able to smuggle in a steady supply of marijuana. They were not only smoking it daily, but supplying most of the work crew with it. Commissary items were the barter, although cash and sex were traded for drugs as well. One day I came back to my cell after the morning meal and found one of my cell mates smoking a joint. He and I had a discussion about his decision to smoke marijuana in our cell. He soon began making better choices. I don't believe he stopped smoking the drug; he just did in other places.

Eventually, the whole ring of dopers got caught. The snitches did their thing, the cells were searched, everything was turned upside down, the contraband was confiscated, and people got written up. The real fun came when each prisoner was interviewed by Captain Lutz.

When my turn came, two officers came to my cell and escorted me to the security office for an interview. The captain told me that she did not believe that I was involved in any of the shenanigans but did believe that I knew who was and she wanted me to tell her. I denied knowing anything. I told her that the other prisoners didn't tell me anything because they knew of my background. She kept insisting that I knew things and I kept denying it. While I was being untruthful, I rationalized that for me to give up any information about anything would seal the deal for my death. I reasoned that I already had a tough jacket to wear; I didn't need any more hassles. I stuck to my guns and she relented. In the aftermath, a bunch of people got locked up and eventually transferred to other prisons. The games didn't stop; the players just changed.

For me, the best way for me to do time was to distract myself in as many ways as I could. I welcomed visits from my family, my wife, and her family, although many times I felt intense shame and guilt about being in this place and having done what I did. Visits from my attorneys helped; Mike Beale was always so positive and helped tremendously to rehabilitate my self-image. Whenever he visited, he observed everything and had tons of questions about the people, processes, and the realities of prison life. I can't help but think that each time he left he was grateful for not living there.

My perception is that all time in prison is Hard Time. Prison is a horrible, dangerous, hopeless place no matter where you are. There are some levels of confinement that are more difficult than others, but doing time is just tough.

Being able to work at night when the majority of people were asleep was great. I had no real supervisor and I felt good about myself because I was providing something to both the prisoners who were working various overnight details, and the security officers who watched over everyone. One security officer was a devout Christian. He and I had many conversations about God, forgiveness, and redemption. Being in prison, I was so skeptical about how God could care for me, but this CSO made it better by helping me to understand that God was able to love me, even when I made stupid choices. One female security officer would come down to the kitchen just to check on me. She told me that she didn't believe what I had done merited the degree of punishment that I got. I think she was on a personal mission to make sure I was protected; on the other hand, she could have been checking to make sure that I wasn't doing anything stupid with their food. Who knows?

My favorite security officer was a former policeman from Mississippi; JoBee was close to 35 years old and was very easygoing in speech and mannerisms. I could tell that he could handle himself physically because he stood close to six feet tall and had that command presence that I recognized right away. Jobee's most outstanding feature was his scarred face. He told me that in an attempt to arrest someone he had taken the spray of a shotgun blast to his face. This man survived that encounter and left police work as a result.

JoBee and I had many conversations and he too expressed his condolences about the way my law enforcement career had ended. He told me that he immediately recognized that I was former law enforcement, and that in his not-so-humble estimation I did not belong in this dangerous place. He confided that he had taken it upon himself to advocate on my behalf to other officers for added security and safety. I was very appreciative of both his words and his presence in my life.

Several months passed without too much drama and then a new dynamic arose. Several of the security officers were transferred, quit, or whatever, and nearly an entire new group of security officers replaced those departed. The relationship between convicted felons and the security force is at best tenuous. Security officers will tell you that prisons are at best organized chaos, and the ability of the prisoners to manipulate the system is only limited by their imagination. Providing security for themselves, civilian employees, and the weaker, older, infirm or otherwise compromised prisoners is a tough, under-appreciated, and difficult task. I was watching this relationship and resultant conditions with a high degree of interest and I believe I was able to learn a great deal about human behavior from observing, participating, and reflecting upon the numerous interactions I had during my confinement.

The majority of the new security crew appeared to me to be younger than the people they were replacing, and there were some notable changes in the way routine interactions were conducted. In an effort to "earn their chops," these newer security officers began systematically changing routines that had been previously established. I noticed this when I was finishing my shift one morning and was braced by a security officer who informed me that I was out of uniform. My "uniform" consisted of a blue chambray shirt, blue jeans, and standard issue brogans for footwear. Since I worked preparing food, I was required to wear a hair net (I actually had hair then). As I was leaving the kitchen that day I had on my hair net, a white T-shirt, blue jeans, and a pair of tennis shoes. This guy was all over me about the lack of the long sleeved, blue chambray shirt. I told him that this was an acceptable adaptation to the uniform regulations because I worked in the kitchen during the overnight shift. He would have none of it and informed me that if he saw me dressed this way again I would be written up. I acknowledged his directive and told him that I would comply. He went on for another several minutes about the whys and wherefores of his approach. I had this nagging feeling in the back of my mind that this would be trouble.

Additionally, there was a new procedure for chow time. The previous routine was fairly basic. Each pod had a scheduled time for chow. If you wanted to eat you went to the chow hall at your prescribed time and secured from the area when the prescribed time was over. The new routine called for the door leading to the chow hall to be secured and everyone was required to line up in the cramped hallway where the security officers would perform inspection for uniform violations. If violations were detected then the offending party would be sent back to his cell to address the violation while all the others waited.

The break from the old routine required adjustment and the specter of public castigation for uniform or other violations created a great deal of tension. Added to this already burgeoning tension was the fact that the resident worker group was now being required to commingle in the new "line up for chow" procedure with prisoners who were HIV positive. This line up occurred in a cramped, poorly lit hallway where there was forced close contact with others and little if any room for movement to safety should trouble arise. I had an intuitive sense that this procedure was going to bring problems for everyone, and it didn't take a genius to figure that out.

After a couple weeks of this kind of change to routines, the pressure, stress, and tightness were overtly profound. Everyone was on edge and verbal squabbling between prisoners, as well as increased verbal sparring with security officers, were nearly constant conditions.

One Sunday afternoon after visitation had ended I found myself alone in the cell because most of my cellmates were working to prepare the evening meal in the kitchen. My cell door was open. I had turned the television on and was watching a football game when I observed two security officers walk down the hallway toward the area where the HIV positive prisoners were housed. I thought nothing of this because security officers walking around together was a common occurrence. Soon I heard a loud conversation coming from down the hall. Though unable to discern the words, the rhythm of this conversation told me that there was some kind of conflict, likely between the security officers and one of the prisoners. The give-and-take continued for some time and then all hell broke loose. Now there were many voices all raised to the hollering/yelling level and there seemed to be no end in sight. While I was mildly curious, I resisted the urge to step over to the open cell door and peer down the hallway; even as this confrontation continued I must have had an intuitive sense not to be drawn into this encounter.

In the next instant, I heard the distinct sound of flesh striking flesh, and what I believed to be a body or /bodies thudding off the steel bulkhead. There was an ever so slight pause followed immediately by the unmistakable sounds of a melee. Bodies bouncing everywhere, yelling, and the crack of leather on flesh. Instantly there was a charge of security officers flying down the hallway past my open cell door to where the fighting was. This contingent was followed by another charge of officers; the riot was in full swing. I could hear the blows being struck, people yelling, glass breaking, and several of the occupants of the cells adjacent to mine beginning either to filter down the hallway toward the fighting, or up toward the chow hall to get further away. It was now time for me to act.

I got up from my bunk and walked over to the cell door and pulled it shut and locked; this heavy solid steel door was equipped with a small chicken wire, reinforced, window that afforded me the view of another wave of security officers racing down the hallway toward the fight. With my cell door closed, the sounds were substantially muffled, but I could definitely hear the commotion down the hall. It lasted for nearly an hour. Several more waves of security officers joined the fray, and eventually medical personnel arrived. In short order, several of the combatants were shackled with foot, hand, and belly chains and led away, likely to be segregated next door at Alhambra Prison.

I alternated between watching the football game, playing chess against the computer, and eyeballing the hallway. I felt safe and secure alone in my cell and was grateful for the fact that I was not in any way involved in this mess. I also wondered how the security officers protected themselves in a fight with folks who were HIV positive. I recall thinking that I would not want to be in such a position.

While watching the game, I heard the familiar sound of a key being placed into the locking mechanism of my cell door. Through the small window I saw JoBee's face; I was instantly grateful that he was not injured. He had a huge smile on his face as he slid the heavy door open. In that slow Mississippi drawl he offered "Now y'all had the right idea now didn't ya?" I looked at him smiling and told him the score of the football game. He nodded knowingly, still grinning from ear to ear. "You OK?" I asked. And he said that he was even though there had been a little excitement. I told him that I was glad that he had not been hurt. He told me that he had to get back to business but had come to check on me. I sat back down as he left and locked the door.

The prison was instantly thrust into "lock down" status. In this case, they kept the workers who had been off the unit in one group and all of those who had been on the unit were locked down. Evening chow would be delayed and it was likely that I would not eat that night. My cell mates, who I learned later were kept in the kitchen, played cards and ate while the investigation of this situation played out. While I was relatively comfortable alone in my cell, I was hungry. Someone placed a cheeseburger and fries from a local fast food chain on the metal trap built into the door of my cell; I have no idea who did this but I was very grateful.

Several members of the Investigation Squad arrived. These folks were dressed in civilian clothes and were there to determine what happened and what charges should be filed against whom. They were accompanied by Wardens Stan Bates (Alhambra) and Jim McFadden (Flamenco). It wasn't long before I was interviewed about what I had observed.

I don't recall the name of the investigator who initially interviewed me. He came to my cell, opened the door, left it open, and told me that he was there to get a statement from me about what I had witnessed. This fellow stood at least six foot two. He wore a sport coat, white collared shirt with no tie, gray trousers, and black shoes. He had a very condescending manner about him. I detected an over-inflated sense of self, coupled with the mind-set that he was holding all the aces in this situation. His approach was to literally stand and look down on me.

Very quickly into the interview he acknowledged that I had been a police officer. Now he didn't do this in a connecting sort of way; it was more along the lines of "you used to be an investigator, but now I'm investigating and I'm in control." It was actually comical because what he didn't know was that I had intentionally not observed anything of substance. I couldn't tell him who did or even said what. I only heard things, and saw security officers running down the hall. When I told him that once I heard the fighting I had closed and locked my cell door he got really pissed off. "You mean to tell me that you just got up, walked over here and shut that door without even glancing down that hallway," he shouted. I told him that was it. "I don't believe you, nobody would do that" was his retort, in the same loud voice. I had mixed emotions at this point; the cell door being open was a huge factor. This interview was basically being broadcast to everyone in the unit. Now having my truthful answers heard by everyone was a good thing; however, even talking with this guy could have had negative implications later. I was starting to get scared and physically stood up to punctuate my responses. I emphatically stated, "Yes, that's what I'm telling you…I never once looked down that hallway throughout the entire ordeal." He was in the middle of telling me that he thought I was lying when Wardens Stan Bates and Jim McFadden entered the cell.

After closing the cell door both wardens greeted the investigator and me. "What's happening here?" Mr. Bates asked. I was thinking about how I was going to hide the computer chess set from Warden McFadden, so when I didn't answer, the investigator started out with, "This *inmate* is trying to convince me that he didn't see anything." I don't know why but the word inmate still rankles me today, and the way this man used it the full derisiveness, contempt, and mocking nature of his tone was evident as he sneered at me.

"What happened, Hal?" asked Mr. Bates. When I recounted what I had done, Mr. Bates looked at Mr. McFadden, arched his eyebrows as if to ask "What do you think?" Mr. McFadden looked at me, at the television with the game still on, at the chess set, and then looked at Mr. Bates and the investigator and said, "You know if he says he didn't look down that hallway I believe him."

While everyone was trying to figure out what to do next, we were interrupted by a knock on the cell door. Through the window I saw JoBee, no smile, all business, clipboard in his hand. The door was unlocked and JoBee addressed both wardens. "The count is done, everyone is accounted for." Warden McFadden responded "Thank you officer, do you happen to have a record of any contact with this prisoner?" Still responding in a business-like tone and manner, JoBee flipped through some papers on the clipboard and responded, "Nevitt was found to be watching television, with the cell door closed and locked, at such and such a time." As he looked from face to face with the two wardens he also said. "I opened the door to check on Nevitt's welfare and at that time he told me that he had closed and locked the door to protect himself from the rioting inmates, and that he had not looked or gone out into the hallway as a safety measure." Both wardens then looked to the investigator who sighed, sneered at me again, and left the cell. JoBee then left to return to whatever he had to do. Both wardens turned to leave and Mr. McFadden turned back to me as he was stepping into the hallway--"nice chess set" was all he said.

I spent nearly one year at Flamenco. I learned so very much from my time there. As the months had passed, ever so slowly, I began to notice a subtle change in me. I noticed that I was not so angry at myself, nor at those whom I had perceived had wronged me. Now I wasn't all the way there yet; forgiveness of self and others wasn't at hand, but I believe I was moving in that direction. The ironic part is that I'm not sure I knew it. My 12-Step sponsor Bill had me reading, writing, and talking about my experiences. Just calling them experiences was quite a change because I had previously referred to my life as "What happened *to me.*" I referred to this as though I was some sort of passive victim who was beset by tragedy. The truth is that I contributed to my condition by the choices I made, and I was now in the process of digesting the entirety of that concept. This is simple stuff, but not necessarily easy. I had continued my meeting attendance, meeting with my sponsor, and working my way through the steps of the program, and I began the process of making amends or mending fences as my sponsor called it.

At this point, I was transferred back to Alhambra and the end of my time in prison was ever so slowly coming into sight. I don't know why they transferred me back to Alhambra; in the prison system there is no need to know the "why" I was simply required to respond to the change.

Chapter 17

BASEBALL DAYS IN PRISON

After being transferred back to Alhambra from Flamenco, I had to make a number of adjustments. First, there was an entire influx of new people. This required an instant adjustment. I had to find out who was who, and how life was being run. The Security Force was still the same, under the same captain. There were some new faces, but by and large they were the same people with the same philosophy. I had to get to know the lay of the land so I could survive this transition.

I was assigned to a large dorm-like room that housed a total of 14 of us. My roommate was a very large, very good-natured man from Yuma, Arizona. I will refer to him as Big Jim. He was a driver who delivered things to other prisons. He was soft spoken and had a lot of credibility among the others. When we met, we shook hands, and he immediately impressed me as someone who I could rely on. He motioned for me to follow him outside the room; I followed and we went out onto the main yard. Big Jim introduced himself, and let me know right away that he was aware of my situation. He assured me that I had nothing to fear from him, and that he was willing to help with the transition to Alhambra. He gave me the rundown on all the folks in our room, and I learned that there was another group of 14 or so in the large room next to ours. He told me that the whole crew knew about my coming over to this place the week before it was to happen--another example of how communication in a prison works. Often the inmates are aware of what is coming before anyone else; it's truly amazing. Big Jim was a true blessing; he was genuine enough to talk straight to me about how we would be establishing our relationship. Although I was appreciative of his directness, I was also still wary. In prison, it's easy to label everyone, and it's necessary for survival to see beyond what is presented. What is the angle? Does this really add up to what is being said/done? How do I measure this? I got really good at listening to my internal voice about people and situations. My very life depended upon this, and with Big Jim I had a level of trust; but until I had experience, I maintained appropriate caution.

Soon I was introduced to the others. This group was made up of an interesting assortment of races, ages, and criminal backgrounds. There were thieves, drug dealers, armed robbers, cop beaters, multiple DUI offenders, and a host of other types of offenders. Each had a unique personality and approach to doing time. Over the time I had remaining, I would come to know each of these people in different ways.

I was initially assigned to be the outside gardener, meaning I worked out in the front of the prison daily. I cut the grass, watered the trees, and tended to plants and flowers. My job was to keep the front of the prison in pristine condition. I was told that Alhambra was the showcase prison and it needed to reflect that image to families, visitors, and dignitaries who came to visit. This was actually the best job I had while I was in prison. First, I worked outside the walls. It was an awesome feeling just to be outside those red brick walls to see traffic, people, dogs, cats, winos, anything at all that would afford an alternate view of the world. Second, I was working with plants, trees, flowers, and grass. I hadn't much experience doing that sort of work, but I was willing to try and this job afforded me the opportunity to affect something in a positive way each day. Eventually, I was assigned an assistant, a fellow who was a farmer in Yuma, Arizona, and who had been convicted of several DUI's. He taught me a lot about watering plants, and how to nurture life out of things that grow from the ground. He also taught me a lot about acceptance, particularly of myself. His easygoing manner and acceptance of everything and everyone was instructive to me and went a long way toward helping me accept that my behavior did not define me as a human being.

This job also had a bit of a down side. Because I worked outside the walls daily, I was in a position to retrieve contraband for those on the inside. I was initially approached by an inmate who simply asked if I would be willing to retrieve a package left by a visitor at visitation. I declined this request and the next time I was not asked but rather told that a package would be delivered the next weekend during visitation, and if I wanted to keep my health record intact I would retrieve the package and turn it over. I still can't remember why I chose to respond by simply stating that I wasn't interested in their business and that I wouldn't mind mixing it up with any or all of them that were gathered, but I did and the threat dissipated. I was scared for a while though.

Thankfully, I only lasted another month or so in that job and was then transferred to the motor pool. This change came about as the result of a couple of guys approaching the two supervisors of the motor pool to let me work there. One was a drug dealer from Phoenix, and the other was a guy who nearly killed someone in a bar fight in a rural Arizona town. These two guys were the first two that I met after Big Jim; they were both assigned to the room I lived in. Our initial contact was such that they just walked up to me on the yard and told me that they knew all about me. Again, I had to assess their intentions and I soon learned that, more than anything, they were curious about how I had stayed alive thus far. Both had come from Perryville Prison, and had heard about "the ex-cop"; their experience with prison was such that they could not believe that someone hadn't killed me yet, so they wanted to know what I was doing, who I knew, and who was protecting me and why? It was freaky because they truly believed I was some kind of bad-ass or something, and I really didn't have credible answers for them. It was upon this basis that I established relationships with these two men, Joe and Davy. Joe was older and had a gravelly, low voice. He was quite a philosopher and a great chess player, though not as good as Karl. We played chess all the time and talked about life, being in prison, what it was going to be like for each of us once we got out, and the importance of being able to decline offers to engage in substance abuse and other activities that appeared attractive but lead to misery.

Davy was a trip. He was a drug dealer who had most of the answers and was looking for a way to get the rest of them. He had an angle for just about everything--a true hustler. For instance, when they put a pool table in the recreation area, he immediately seized upon the opportunity to run a 9-ball tournament for money. Now money in prison is a valuable commodity, and strictly prohibited by rule. That doesn't mean there wasn't any. The game was played in the open, and the money exchanged after the game. Davy enlisted the aid of a partner and subtly they began to clean up on the unsuspecting "fish" who joined the game. It was incredible to watch as Davy's partner would mix making shots and missing to set up Davy for the score shots on the 5 and 9 balls. They never did get caught, but Big Jim knew what was happening and single-handedly disrupted the con with a direct conversation with the both of these men wherein he made it clear that they would be better off by discontinuing this practice.

One of the other guys was Bobby. He was a statewide driver who had an effusive, enthusiastic, folksy manner. He was imprisoned for some sort of theft and was one of the most positive individuals I have ever met. We would eventually collaborate on creating a softball team, a process that was truly miraculous.

Our first job was to get permission to form the team. This was actually risky business for the employees of that prison. One of their primary concerns was how to keep the inmate population off balance. This is actually necessary for employee survival. Any sort of prisoner alliance is not only noted, but measures had to be taken to dilute the power of such alliances or employees could face dire consequences up to and including death. The prospect of forming a softball team within the walls of Alhambra Prison created some political and tactical challenges for everyone concerned.

This then was a job for Major Bauer. He was as intelligent, fair-minded, and non-political as any human being I have ever met. He was initially approached by Bobby and Davy; the major loved the idea and immediately assigned Frank C., a huge, Hispanic, transportation officer to sponsor, supervise, and manage the team. Frank and I played on the Department of Public Safety Football Team together, so this was a great turn of events.

Once assigned, Frank met with all of the resident workers and let us all know his expectations. There would be practice every day but Sunday, two hours rain or shine; each individual was expected to address the issue of getting into physical condition for playing softball. Any rule infraction would be grounds for automatic dismissal from the team; furthermore, all team members, and the team itself were under the microscope of the factions that did not want the team to be in place. Thus, we were all targets and had to be straight arrow all the way or the team would be dissolved immediately. This would take on additional significance later when we got authorization to play in tournaments in the community, but for now we all had to be aware of what we were getting into as it related to life in the prison. I came away from that initial meeting very excited. The prospect of having a goal, and a mission that involved working with others was unbelievably energizing. I saw hope on the faces of those who previously had none, and I have come to believe that is one of the most sacred moments we as humans can experience.

At that initial meeting, Frank assigned Davy, Bobby, and me to be team captains, and we scheduled a meeting with Major Bauer to discuss the matter of practicing, equipment, and other such details. In those days, immediately east of the Alhambra Reception Center, a maximum security prison, was an abandoned baseball field overgrown with weeds, the turf was uneven, and trash was strewn across the entire field; it was in a general state of disrepair. It would need a lot of work. This was going to be a challenge because the field was outside the prison, protected only by a chain link fence. This would be a security nightmare. Drugs, money, weapons, and other contraband could easily be passed over or even through this fence, thus putting inmates, correctional service officers, and others at risk. The person or persons assigned to repair this field would have to be of the appropriate security classification; they would need to be trustworthy to work out in that field, mostly unsupervised, for extended periods each day. And there was another requirement-- whoever was to perform this work would also need to be able to operate a front loading tractor.

Bobby and I approached Major Bauer on the main yard at Alhambra. As the three of us walked and talked, it became apparent that the Major was going to assign me to the task of clearing the field. As we walked out of the rear of the prison, the Major looked at me and asked "You know how to drive that tractor don't you." The old steel gray tractor was parked outside the field. To this day, I have no idea what kind it was; I just know that I had no earthly idea of how to drive it, or much more how to operate the front end loader. I just know that Bobby was nodding his head up and down furiously, out of the Major's sight, as the seconds, which seemed like hours, passed before I answered the question. "Sure" I said, as he turned to go back inside, "Then get it done, I'll let security know you'll be assigned to this detail." As he went back inside he was all smiles and his whooping could be heard by all of Phoenix I'm sure. Bobby, who knew this tractor inside out, gave me an in-service on how to operate the beast; he also told me that it was old, and had a hydraulic leak-- whatever that meant--but I could get past all that by refilling it every day. I became a tractor driver in a matter of minutes.

So the next day, I went outside the back of the prison, started up the tractor as per Bobby's instructions, and began to clear the field. Though there were many stops and starts, I spent two weeks riding this tractor, pulling weeds, clearing trash, and basically making the field playable. Each day, prisoners and future teammates in transit from Alhambra to other places on the compound would wave, whistle, and cheer as they saw the transformation of the field. In those first few days, Major Bauer stayed away, thankfully, as I was learning how to drive the tractor that I allegedly already knew how to drive; but then he would appear daily, sometimes joined by the warden, sometimes with security staff, and at times with people I didn't know or recognize.

The time spent driving around that field in the daily sun that is Arizona was peaceful, calming, and, in many ways, soothing to my soul. I could give myself respite from the terrible feelings of guilt, shame, and remorse of the conduct that got me into prison. Just as important was the fact that I now had a goal, and in a big way others were depending on me to get this project done so we could have a place to play ball. In many ways, clearing this field was a parallel to clearing the field of my mind. Truth be told, my mind needed clearing as well as remolding. I had become a selfish, self-centered, egotistical user of people, places, and things, and for me to have any type of life, I needed to reorder priorities, learn coping and living strategies, and, more than anything, develop a purpose for my life. Perhaps not so strangely, driving a tractor around a dilapidated softball field provided me with plenty of opportunity to come to grips with the idea that my life needed some drastic changes. I needed to level the field of my mind and soul; clear away the weeds, trash, and useless baggage and disasters of my past; and, most importantly, backfill the empty space with thoughts, principles, and a plan for effective living.

Incidentally, the process of clearing the dirt field was not without some problems. Lost in thought, and lacking experience, I dug up too much dirt, and we actually had to have some backfill brought in. But, in the end, it was a fabulous experience for me, and one that I will not forget.

After the two weeks, the field was inspected by Major Bauer, Frank C., and the warden of the prison. They all congratulated me on completing the job and once the warden left we began to formulate a practice schedule, and a way to select a team.

Several of the resident workers had been doing conditioning drills, and most of us were in decent shape. We got softballs, and gloves, bats, and other equipment were kept by Frank, and we started practicing every day after evening chow. It was quite a spectacle watching guys who had varying degrees of athletic ability try to form a team. I learned so much about principles versus personalities as well as seeing this group of convicted felons become vulnerable with respect to their individual and collective ability to formulate attitudes, values, and behaviors that had very little to do with playing softball, but had so much to do with self-concept, sacrifice, and human dignity. I was amazed daily at how this group could function effectively, then fail, regroup, and function effectively again. There were several tense moments when people mucked up situations, and the reactions among convicts were swift, direct, and often times less than esteem building. But we got through, and after a couple of weeks of practice were ready for our first game.

The softball games began when Frank contacted Grace Community Church in Tempe, Arizona, and they agreed to come play us. The deal was they would come to the prison and play the softball game, and after the game they would "witness to us" about their God/church experience. The anticipation for this first game was almost unbearable. We actually got uniforms that were fantastic and when the big day arrived everyone was excited. When the other team arrived, they were clad in only team shirts but we had actual uniform pants, shirts, and hats, all paid for out of some sort of inmate recreation fund. We looked great. They kicked our ass in the game. It was obvious they had played together awhile. Afterward we sat on the bleachers and listened to these guys talk about God. The whole experience was surreal in that for me the coming together of this group was next to impossible, yet here we were playing ball, and interacting in a somewhat meaningful way with members of society. What an absolute trip. Thus began our foray into athletic competition and interaction with people from the "world."

After they left the field, we were then herded into processing and strip searched by a select squad of correctional service officers. This was the official act of protest by Captain Jim McClelland, one of the many Security Personnel who opposed the formation of this team. His handpicked squad subjected us to group strip searches after every game; while prison security was necessary, the people in charge of this appeared to delight in the degradation and humiliation of this group. To me this appeared to be their way of maintaining control of the inmates. The irony here is that as a group we made it clear that any attempt to introduce contraband would be met with swift retribution; the prison administration and security force would be the least of any offender's concerns.

This team eventually evolved into quite a spectacle. We played several church teams in the beginning and actually won some games. We came together as a group, and learned a lot about cooperation, teamwork, and sacrifice. We probably learned something about God and the people who had successfully integrated the concept into their lives. We eventually were able to enter softball tournaments off the prison grounds and spent several weekends playing ball in various parts of the state of Arizona. To my knowledge, there was never any use of prohibited substances, nor any attempt to introduce contraband. There was a rumor that between some of the games instances of commingling with attending spouses/significant others occurred; however, this was never proven and likely just a rumor.

Eventually, word about this team reached other prisons within the state of Arizona and soon a challenge was issued by the group out a Perryville, which is a prison located on the western edge of Phoenix. The challenge was accepted, a date and time arranged, and most were excited about the prospect of playing another prison team. I was excited too, but I also had a sense of foreboding. In fact, I was scared to go there. I had never been to Perryville, but I intuitively knew that this could be a venture into danger. Who was there that knew me? What security measures were there? Who would be allowed to watch the game? All of these thoughts and many more went through my head as the date neared. Frank and Major Bauer would be there, but would that be enough?

On the hour-long bus ride out there I was anxious, but didn't want anyone to know. I prayed. I tried to calm myself. I tried to visualize what it would be like to be on that yard with all those people and what if someone recognized me? Who would stand up for me? What if something got started--how would I stay alive?

Once we got there, we were searched prior to going in. We were led to a field much more modern than ours. They even had white chalk lines and batters boxes. They had new dugouts and a backstop. We started warming up and then the Perryville team came; we all got introduced and things looked pretty good. Then a slow steady stream of prisoners began to make their way to this field. I got an uneasy feeling about this but nothing happened until I came up to bat.

As I made my way to the batter's box, someone in the crowd began wailing like a siren. It was subtle at first, but then it got more intense. I started to get really freaked out. I did manage to hit the ball harder than I ever have before and while running the bases I spotted the guy in the crowd doing the yelling. It was clear that he had made me, and was letting others know who I was by making the siren noise. I was involved in a play at the plate and after sliding in, I saw him looking directly at me making the noise, and saying "That's him, that's Nevitt." The weird thing was that nobody seemed to be paying attention at first. My teammates were unaware of the situation, but I was simply terrified. There were about 500 prisoners out watching this game, and it seemed like 5,000.

I stood apart from my teammates trying to figure out what to do. It would only be a matter of time before this situation turned really ugly. I had a metal bat in my hands and just stood watching the guy. He stared back at me with a malevolent grin on his face; he knew he had the advantage.

One of my teammates approached me. "What's going on with you?" he asked. I feigned nothing being wrong, and he astutely responded, "bullshit." "You haven't let go of that bat ever since you got over here, and you have a really mean look on your face. What's happening?"

I told him about the dude and the siren noise. He laughed when he realized how serious this situation was for me. He told me to come with him. We both walked over to Davy; he was not only one of our Team Captains, but had been on the Perryville Yard for a couple of years, and was well acquainted with the guys playing on the Perryville team. We explained the situation to Davy; he got really pissed off when he heard what was happening. He told me to stay with him and to follow him when the inning was over. When that happened, we trotted over to the Perryville team captain, a guy I didn't know named Griffey, who stood about six two, and was a good 250 pounds. He had a hard face that belied no emotion at all. He was definitely in command and apparently was a friend of Davy's. Davy told him who I was, and what was happening in the stands. Griffey looked at me, sized me up, and with a sandpaper rough voice said, "You got some kinda balls to even come in here, we'll handle that guy for ya." He looked at Davy and said "If this goes bad take your guys to the outfield, my guys will join you...this could be fun." I really liked his spirit, and the fact that he was willing to help endeared him to me as well.

What happened next was one of the most amazing things I have ever seen in my entire life. Our entire team met between first base and the pitcher's mound. Davy briefed the guys about what was happening. I watched across the field as Griffey and his crew met. As we took the field, the guys from our team that weren't playing all picked up bats, and very subtly placed themselves between the bad guy and me. Griffey waded into the crowd and emerged with two of the largest lads I have ever seen. The two giants made their way over to the first base side of the crowd and after a brief conversation with the bad guy convinced him to join them for a short walk away from the field. The last I saw of him, he was walking very slowly and talking very quickly to his newly acquired escorts. I never saw him, nor heard from him again.

I don't remember who won the game, but I do remember how deeply grateful I felt for the support of my own guys, and a group of guys I did not know. This event was nothing short of miraculous. I don't believe any of the meager security force was even aware of the non-incident that occurred. Without planning it, or discussing it beforehand, two differing groups met on a field of competition and in the spirit of allowing for that competition took a stand for the concept of a principle versus a personality or personalities. For a brief moment on that field the universe posed a question to some people, and they responded in an honorable fashion. In a place where one would not expect to find honor, it was there. I saw it; no, I experienced it, with every fiber of my being and its everlasting impression has never left my memory.

When the game was over I remember shaking hands with all the guys from the other team. Hearing them respond with words of acceptance and inclusion was a great experience. I know that it may sound strange to be gratified by acceptance from a group of prisoners. In the moments that comprised that day we shed our labels. For a period of time, we were simply human beings gathered together for a purpose; and when one person sought to degrade that process, the two groups came together in one accord and made a choice to act honorably. In the aftermath, their kind words were noticed, and appreciated, but the words paled in comparison to what they did. They stood up for a man whom they did not know, yet the overriding principle was to allow someone the freedom to be who they were; judgments about the past were put aside. I learned a valuable lesson that day, and remain truly grateful for having experienced that.

The bus ride back was a raucous affair because I was razzed about playing third base, and running the bases armed with a metal bat. I stood up on that bus and thanked each of my teammates for their willingness to stand beside me, even when it meant exposure to threats from some of the planet's most dangerous people. I learned a lot that day; perhaps the most important issue was the fact that if those guys could stand up for me perhaps I wasn't as morally bankrupt as I had imagined myself to be.

Chapter 18

THE CIVIL TRIAL

During my second year in prison, the civil trial began for the shooting that had occurred on Valentine's Day in 1986. I had been participating in legal visits with Mike Beale, my attorney, throughout the two years leading up to the trial, including a videotaped deposition that was conducted in the visitation room at the Alhambra Prison. The deposition consisted of me being asked questions by legal counsel for the family of the man I had shot and killed. Even during the deposition, I was emotionally overcome when I recounted the events that occurred on that day to the extent that I needed to take time out during the questioning because I felt so sad about what I had been required to do in defense of my life.

Prior to the trial date being set I received a visit from several officers from Scottsdale P.D. Prison security arranged for us to have a secluded room for the purpose of this visit. I recall with gratitude being in that room with a group of my former teammates. We ate pizza and talked about the old times we had together. It was exactly what I needed prior to a wrongful death trial. I want to give a special Thank You from my heart to all who visited me on that day and who took time out to come to that prison to see me. I am and will remain eternally grateful for that!

As the trial date approached, Mike came and visited me and we worked with the security staff to schedule transport and security issues for getting me back and forth from court. Each day, I attended the trial and was escorted by a plain clothes security officer. I was allowed to wear a suit because the jury did not know that I was imprisoned.

On the first day of trial, I was escorted by Major Bauer. I recall getting to the courthouse and standing out in the hallway when Daniel M. Sr. arrived, he was the father of the deceased. He strode right up to me, within less than a foot from my face and just stared at me without saying a word. We both remained silent just staring at one another when Major Bauer barked at him to move along, a command that he complied with.

I listened intently as Mike Beale addressed the jury. He at one point stood right in front of the jury box and pointed directly at me and said: "You need to ask yourselves, if you were in the same position would you do the same thing that that guy right there did?" I sat at the table barely breathing, looking at each of the jurors and trying to figure out how they were reacting. I listened as the experts testified as to use of force dynamics and how I responded appropriately to the threat presented by a man running toward me with a gun in his hand.

At the lunch break each day, I would eat lunch at a nearby restaurant with my mom, and an escort from the Arizona Department of Corrections. The lawyers would go wherever they would go and we would reconvene after lunch and listen to more testimony from witnesses.

At the end of each day, I would return to Alhambra State Prison and resume my life as a prisoner. Most days, I would go immediately to softball practice, already in progress. And each day the team would gather round and demand a description of the days' events in court. This was my life, and these were the people in it--a group of prisoners who supported one of their own through an obviously tough time. That was a special group; they were people who would normally not mix socially, occupationally, or in any other situation. But here in this setting we were just men dealing with life as it presented itself on a daily basis.

I heard Daniel M. Sr. testify that he observed his son walk up to me and try to hand me the gun; at which time, he observed me pull my pistol and shoot his son several times without being threatened by him. As I listened to that I recall the extreme shame that I experienced just thinking that someone could say that about me. Here I was in prison for criminal behavior, and this man was saying things that were untrue yet convicted me to my very soul.

I also recall being interviewed in prison by Ben C., a use of force expert and an assistant chief on Phoenix P.D. who eventually became chief of police in a large city in Texas. His testimony in court was favorable to me. He was a very effective witness and I will never forget that he told the court that he noticed that each time I spoke of the incident I became emotional about having to take the life of another human being. Ben and I met several years later when he was on the Board of Governors for the State Bar of Arizona.

When it came time for me to testify, I was so tied up emotionally that I don't know how I was able to give anything resembling coherent testimony. I was experiencing a myriad of thoughts and emotions, from fear to guilt, shame, and a sense of loneliness. I told the court what had happened as I remembered it and, predictably, I cried as I relived the abject terror that I experienced, and the choice I made on that fateful day. When I came off the witness stand I was completely drained, and in that moment I thought that I had fallen woefully short of describing what I had experienced prior to making the decision to pull the trigger.

When the case concluded and the jury began deliberation, I was amazed at how much emotion I still carried. I had experienced the phenomena of my fate being in the hands of a judge several years prior to this, but I had not ever been in the position of having a jury judge my conduct. It was scary. What did they think? How much about me did they actually know? Who did they believe? As these thoughts swirled about in my head I walked in and around building, and I'm sure the assigned escort was annoyed at I walked. I recall seeing two detectives from Scottsdale

P.D. and they waved and yelled to me from their vehicle as they were apparently leaving the courthouse.

After an hour or so (seemed like a lot more), we got word that the jury had reached their verdict and it was time to reconvene. As I stood and faced them my calm demeanor belied the emotional turmoil that was occurring inside of me. The verdict was read and I was found not responsible for Daniel M.'s wrongful death. I felt relieved that the jury had found that I had acted appropriately for that situation. I was certainly grateful that I did not have to pay a huge financial penalty, I was more grateful for the validation of my behavioral response. At the same time, I felt sad that a young man had paid so dearly for his abuse of alcohol on that day of his life.

In the aftermath my lawyer, Mike B., directed me to a small room at the front of the courtroom itself. We spoke briefly and he told me that some members of the press wanted to get a statement from me. We invited them into the room and I made a brief comment about my gratitude for the jury's decision and that my goal was to move on with my life, such as it is. Nearly four years later, when in the process of making amends to the judge who had sentenced me to prison, he asked me what I had meant by the statement about "living my life, such as it is." I told him then that I simply wanted to get out of prison and begin my new life.

As I left the courthouse that day and returned to prison, I felt a sense of relief and gratitude for that aspect of my life having been resolved. And, yes, back at prison on that day I met with the softball team and we all experienced a sense of gratitude for the result in court that day.

Chapter 19

PAROLE HEARING

When I had been transferred back to Alhambra Prison, I was assigned a case manager. His nickname was "Bad-Day." He met with me infrequently and made notes in a file about what I had been doing with my time in prison. He noted that I had taken a few classes, was attending AA meetings regularly, and had been instrumental in putting together a softball team. In one of our more memorable meetings in early 1989, he told me that I would soon be eligible for a parole hearing and that I should begin the process of determining who would attend, what they would say, and what I would say to the Parole Board.

After determining that I was eligible for parole, a hearing was convened at the Alhambra Prison Visitation Room. It sounds funny but I wore my best blue chambray shirt, my best blue jeans, and my red and white ankle high basketball shoes. The Parole Board consisted of three panel members who wore suits and ties and looked very professional. Thinking back, it now seems so ridiculous that I was sitting there in my jeans and tennis shoes.

Major Bauer had agreed to talk to the Board, and in fact had written a letter in favor of my being granted parole. My mother and father testified, as did Pete Wooster, a police officer from Scottsdale P.D. I was really, really scared. I wanted out of that place so bad and these folks were able to make that happen for me.

Major Bauer spoke first; he told them that he didn't believe I should have been given such a harsh sentence in the first place. He told them that I had adjusted well to the adversity, and had tried my best to fit in and do the best with the time. He spoke of how I had attended AA meetings regularly, and how I had been instrumental in arranging for inmate enrichment through participation in a softball team. This team had played local churches in exchange for them giving us a message of salvation. The Major was a very impressive witness, and I was certainly glad that he was on my side on this one.

My mother and father testified that it was time for me to come home; both were terrific. I remember that my father was close to tears, and I had never seen that before! I was overcome with guilt and shame again after seeing that.

Pete Wooster basically told them that he would take custody of me if they released me to work for him. He and another officer had started a business and I was to be their employee. He was most impressive, and he left them with the idea that there was no question in his mind that releasing me was the right thing to do, and they would not be disappointed by my behavior upon release.

I talked to the Board as well. They asked about my crimes, and I remember facing the facts. I told them that I had been an undercover narcotics detective, and the plain truth is that I had used cocaine on an early narcotics buy, and that I liked that drug so much that I began using it on a regular basis. In that moment, I felt relieved to be able to say it so clearly and plainly.

They asked about programming in prison, and I detailed how I had gone to as much schooling as was allowed. There had been some security concerns, so I had been restricted from some courses due to threats to my safety. They asked about the softball team, and I recounted that. I also told them that my goals were to go to college, earn a degree, and help others who encountered drug addiction and other life problems.

When I left the room, I felt like my effort had fallen so short of getting the salient points across to the Board members. They looked like statues as they listened patiently; they gave no indication as to whether they believed in what had been presented to them, or not. I had no idea which way they would vote.

Mike, one of the Department of Corrections officers, was present for the hearing and stayed after as the Board discussed each case presented. He escorted me out of the hearing room, and stopped me before opening the door out to the yard. He said, "Hal, you did a great job in there; I agree with The Major, you shouldn't have been made to endure this deal." I was absolutely stunned; these guys, while human, have a tough job, and it's not common for them to offer any opinions about prisoners' lives, or such things as what is or is not deserved. This was an unusual interchange. He then said that he would be present when they voted on whether or not to grant me parole, and would notify me as soon as he knew. About 2 hours later (it seemed like a day and a half), he called by phone over to the Motor Pool and notified me that the board had voted 3-1 in favor of granting me parole!! I was ecstatic!!! I would be going home soon!!

Not soon enough obviously. For the first three years, the days dragged as though the clock was frozen. After the parole hearing, the days were so agonizingly slow that I nearly lost my mind. The days consisted of me going to my assigned work area at the motor pool hoping that I would get a call that it was time to go. None came for nearly a month. I became convinced that my paperwork had been lost, that I had been charged with something else, or that I was simply never going to be released and would be in this state of limbo for the rest of my life. I would return from the motor pool each day and go directly to the security office. The supervisors knew and they would look at me and shake their heads no. I would then return to my room and do the process all over again the next day.

On the day I was released, the afternoon was just like any other. I had worked all day at the motor pool with the constant thought: "Will this be the day?" At about 3:00 in the afternoon, I walked back to the main prison. I had to come through the back gate and get buzzed through the enormous door. The irony here is that I was coming back to the prison, asking to be buzzed through, and yet my whole focus was "when do I get out of here."

After a quick search by the on-duly corrections officer, I was shuttled through the back of the prison, past the kitchen, and through a door onto the main yard. Things were normal. The prisoners from Dog Ward were out on the yard, all dressed in orange jumpsuits; some were walking and talking, some were running, others were tossing a football around. I always looked around, vigilant for some sign of danger. Anyone could be waiting for a chance to kill the ex-cop.

As I walked across the yard to my housing area, I saw that the security office door was open, and some of the officers were milling about. Nothing was unusual about that. Once I made it to the outside door to my living area, I let myself in with my key, and made my way through the lobby to the door to my living area. This room, shared by twelve men, was now dark because I was the only one there. I went to my bunk, laid down, and began to read the newspaper.

One by one, a few of the guys returned to the room, their work day done; they came back to relax before supper. We exchanged greetings casually, and each man returned to his own way of dealing with being locked up one more day. After laying there for several minutes, I heard the outside door open up, and I heard the distinct sound of the footfalls of several officers moving toward the room I was in. What made the sound distinct and recognizable was the sound of the metal chains they carried.

As they came toward the room, I wondered who they were coming for. I had seen this before. Someone had messed up badly and was about to be "arrested" and sent to some sort of disciplinary segregation. I heard the door to the room next to ours being thrust open, and a loud voice boomed "Where's Nevitt?" Another voice responded, but not loud enough for me to hear; I didn't need to hear to know that the voice directed the officers to the room I was in. I was in a near panic. All I could think of was "What had I done?" I was so close to getting out, and now they are coming to arrest me. Now, I knew of cases where people had been charged with additional crimes prior to being released. Could this be happening to me? Who? What? When? All of this went through my mind.

Those thoughts were interrupted by the door being thrust open, and the lights being turned on. Immediately, I saw Officer Vignault; a man in his early 50s whose son was a Phoenix Police Detective. I stood up looking directly at him. He looked at me and in a loud voice said, "Assume the position!" Behind him were at least five more CSO's, all of whom I recognized, all looking serious, grim, and resolute.

I turned, faced my bunk, placed my hands on the top bed, and waited. The entire entourage crossed the room in unison and surrounded me, as my heart beat wildly. One of the other prisoners in the room asked, "What the hell did *he* do?"

Not one of the CSO's answered, they simply gathered around me, while one patted me down and another took my hands off the bed, turned me around, and fixed the body chains to my ankles, waist, and wrists. I was trussed up so tight that I couldn't move; I was shocked. I saw the bewildered looks of the other prisoners; we were all wondering what was going to happen next.

Officer Vignault spoke up. He looked directly at me and said, "Major Bauer says if you can get your stuff packed up by 4:00 you can leave!" I looked around, all the rest of the CSO's began smiling and laughing.

The prisoners joined in. I began hopping around trying to gather up my clothes and other belongings. I nearly fell several times; everyone was having a great laugh watching me go from pure, bewildered fright to exuberant joy!! I was going home after three and one half years in prison.

The chains were soon removed and my roommates were asked to leave the room. The CSO's gathered around and each told me how happy he was that I was leaving. Each in his own way admonished me about coming back, and each in his own way acknowledged that this part of the journey was over.

I gathered up my things, went to the security office, signed some papers, and was escorted out of that place for what I thought was the last time. But I would return to that very prison several years later at the request of a substance abuse counselor. I shared my story with a group of people from the community as we reached out to prisoners. One man, upon his release, actually came to my church several times and was active for a time in the recovering community.

I can say today that I was both happy to leave that place, and happy to return to it for the right reason.

Chapter 20

RELEASED FROM PRISON

On the day that I was released from prison, my mom met me in the parking lot at the State Prison Complex at Alhambra. I had my belongings in boxes and we put them in the trunk of her white Cadillac and simply drove out of that parking lot and went home to Scottsdale. My mind was moving at light speed. My wife was in California at a business conference and her mother and father were watching my then three-year-old son. As we drove through the streets of Scottsdale on the way home, I recalled the events from the past. A veritable kaleidoscope of happenings that shaped and comprised a life; there were a number of happy, satisfying memories, accompanied by a sense of remorse and regret, all of this enveloped in a deep sense of gratitude for being free once again.

I was also beset with fear. That fear that comes from not knowing how my life would be. Convicted felon! How would I get a job? Who would want me to work for them? What kind of work could I do? How would people react to me? Oh yeah, also a constant reminder was the internal dialogue of how my best thinking had earned me a spot in the state penitentiary...what was I gonna do to keep from going back in there? This fear was in some ways greater than the fear that I had when I first got to prison.

As we turned down the street to my parents' home, I observed that one of my childhood friends was out in his driveway working on the car with another guy. They both waved as we passed and I knew that there would be a case of beer in the cooler; and I wondered, if I went for a visit, how I would handle not drinking with them.

My dad greeted us at the door. I was so glad to be home. We had a nice supper and talked about what my plans were for the rest of my life.

After supper, I went outside and walked two houses down where my friends were working on the car. This was the friend with whom I had first gotten drunk at the age of 12. They stopped working on the car and we talked for a bit. It was really awkward. I mean what do you say when you have just been released from prison? How do you reconnect? What about the beer? We stumbled around trying to find stuff to talk about. I managed to refuse the offer of a beer and after a while gave my good-byes and went back to my parents' home. I could see the look of relief on my friends' faces when I left, and it was matched by my mom's when I returned and she was able to see that I had not been drinking. First hurdle cleared. It was now time to go to my house.

Prior to my imprisonment, my wife and I were in the process of buying a brand new home. That dream went by the wayside. She had rented a modest home in Northeast Phoenix. My mom drove me there, and nobody was home because my wife was in California attending a seminar, and my in-laws were taking care of our son. I didn't know where they were but I was able to get into the house. After my mom left, I just sat there and took it all in. A home...there were three-year-old things there, stuff that a baby would need. I was really overwhelmed as I looked around and thought of all that had happened, and more so about what was going to happen.

Prior to leaving the prison, I had called my program sponsor to let him know I was being released. Truth be told I was afraid of what would happen. Would there be press? How would I respond? Being clean and sober in prison was one thing; now I had to road test this new way in the real world. My sponsor was so calm about it; "Get your meeting schedule out, find a meeting near your house, let me know when and where it is and I will come get you and we'll go to the meeting." How simple. I located a meeting that was within blocks of my house. I called him from my house and true to his word he arrived there in time for us to get to the meeting. He brought a man named Ed with him and the three of us went together.

Prior to my sponsor's arrival, my in-laws came home with Kevin. What an ecstatic reunion! Kevin and I hugged, I cried, and we played with all his toys while my in-laws watched. I was absolutely ecstatic, and so was Kevin.

When Bill and Ed pulled up in the driveway the lights shone into the living room. Kevin went to the window and pulled the drapes aside. Bill told me later that both he and Ed commented on seeing that little boy, and then his father framed in that window. They both said that it was worth their time that night just to see our smiling faces looking out from that window.

My mother-in-law and father-in-law, Edie and Bill, were so gracious. They stayed with my son while I went to my first "real world 12-Step meeting." I think it is significant to say that within four hours of being released from prison, I was attending a 12-Step meeting. During my time at Alhambra Prison, I observed first-hand guys being released on parole, and within a week they returned. I had done my informal, anecdotal study of what led them back, and I never, ever heard any of those that returned say that they had called their sponsor and had gone to a 12-Step meeting their first night out. I was really determined not to go back to prison, and not to drink alcohol or use drugs. Going to this first 12-Step meeting was not only necessary for that, it was a real good way for me to get a bit of a handle on all the emotions I was feeling and the thoughts I was having.

The meeting itself was memorable for a couple of reasons. First off, it was in a room that had carpet; I was used to linoleum tile floors in the prison, there was laughter and banter among group members, and my sponsor actually knew some people there. I was elated; I also ran into some guys that I had gone to high school with. This was very interesting and, as it turned out, very educational for me. The meeting was the type where a speaker shared for a brief period, and then we took a smoke break. It was during this smoke break that

I learned about my friends from school. I didn't smoke but I went outside to talk with my former school chums. What I learned from talking to them chilled me to the very core of my being. These guys (4-5 of them) were joking about the fact that they were attending meetings at the behest of their wives, or girlfriends, and weren't really serious about not drinking. This was astounding to me. As I listened to their banter with each other and with me, I learned that each of them was actually drinking in between meetings, and it was actually working for each of them. My mind was working feverishly on this information, and I actually began to think that perhaps I, too, could do what they were doing successfully. Fortunately for me, I was able to snap out of this trance remembering that less than five hours ago I had been released from prison, and a condition of my staying released was not drinking. You would think that this would be so easy to remember, but the strange mental twist that precedes a drink or drinking spree is a very real phenomena and needs to be acknowledged and addressed, at least it did for me.

Thank God I was at a 12-Step meeting when the fantasy of successful drinking came to me; I returned to the meeting and through listening to others was able to dismiss this fantasy without acting on it. It didn't hurt that during the meeting I got tagged/called upon to share my experience, strength, and hope, so without any misgivings I disclosed to the group that I had just been released from prison and was currently on parole with a stipulation that I not drink or use drugs. When the meeting was over, several people came to me and gave me business cards with the sincere admonition to call before I drank. I left that meeting with mixed thoughts and feelings. First and foremost it felt great to leave a meeting and not have to go back to a cell; but what about those people who were just kinda going through the motions, I had some fear about that. Bill and Ed were great. They focused on the fact that the three of us had gone to the meeting and left sober. I did not go back to that meeting for almost three years; I did go to other meetings though, and that was the key for me staying sober. My sponsor suggested strongly that I attend 90 meetings in 90 days, so I set out to do just that.

We returned to my house and I said good-night to two great friends and went inside the house. I got to talk with my mother-in-law and father-in-law for a while before they left for the night. I can't say enough about how gracious they were. This was very awkward for me, but they never expressed any judgment or anger with me for negatively impacting their daughter's and their lives. They were very kind to me and I will never forget that.

The next morning I woke up for the first time in my home. There were no sounds of the jailer's keys, no sounds of slamming metal doors, no sounds of flesh hitting flesh, and no loud voices barking orders. There was simply the sound of peace and quiet that comes from being in a home. To this day, that is still attractive to me. I am extremely grateful for those sounds. Then there was the sound of a three year old boy running into my room; he jumped into my arms, and I knew it was time to start our day together. Wow... what exuberance, excitement, and fun. How wonderful to be in the presence of this boy, and have something to do with him.

Those first few days when my son and I were together were absolute bliss for me--two boys playing, laughing, hugging, rolling on the floor, wrestling, and just being together. We went to the park and played for hours; we played with his toys; he showed me everything--twice! It was just what the doctor ordered for me. I was focused on him and our relationship so much that I never had the thought of drinking or using drugs. Each day as I put him down to bed and got myself ready for sleep I was so thankful to be out of that terrible, lonely, isolated existence in prison. God, in his infinite wisdom, knew that I would need some time to release all those pent up emotions, so he gave me this time with my son, and the scenes from those first few days with just him and me are indelibly etched upon my mind.

During that first week, I also had to go meet my parole officer, Jessie M. I recall how I got dressed up with a shirt and tie that first or second morning out of prison, preparing to go meet this man who would direct my life for the next few years. I was standing in my living room and called his office at 8:00 am sharp. He answered the phone and when I told him that I was preparing to come down to his office he stopped me short. He told me that he appreciated my willingness to contact him, and to come down there that day, but he scheduled visits with his parolees and he had not scheduled my first visit until the next week. I was really puzzled by this. My perception was that I was "Public Enemy Number One" and the whole world would be watching and waiting for me to jump through all the hoops. Jessie was very low key and told me that he had every confidence that I would be successful in my effort to complete work furlough and parole without any problems. We arranged to meet the following week and I was nothing short of amazed at how non-directive this man was.

My wife was not due home until Saturday evening so the week was filled with two boys getting to know each other. One occasion stands out in my mind. We were at the park and had been playing all morning; my son had a limited vocabulary, being only three years old. In the middle of our running, romping, and playing at the park, he stopped suddenly and simply pointed to his mouth; it was approaching mid-day and this child was hungry. Now his father, new to all this, had not planned for this, and he was letting me know that he needed to eat! I laughed about this for weeks. Of course we stopped playing and went home to eat immediately, but I was struck by the irony of this small boy pointing to his mouth to communicate to his father that he was hungry--that was too funny. He and I have both laughed at that more than once throughout our lives.

The first Saturday out I planned to go to an early morning 12-Step meeting at the North Scottsdale Fellowship Club. This decision, as it turns out, was to be truly a life changing event. As I write this today, some twenty plus years later, I still attend that club regularly. For that first meeting, I met my good friend Laura M. at her home at 6:30 am to drop my son off so I could attend the meeting. Laura had told me that she would support my attendance at meetings in whatever way she could. Laura is the older sister of my best childhood friend; she is a great Christian woman and a true friend. I had no misgivings about leaving my son with her while I went to the meeting. Once I arrived at the meeting, the first thing I observed was that I was early, and there were only a few people there. The man who was chairperson of the meeting greeted me and immediately told me "Well if you are gonna be early, you gotta work." As he was speaking, he handed me the paper with the fifth chapter of the Big Book of Alcoholics Anonymous printed on it. The custom is to read this prior to most meetings. I took the paper, found a seat, and waited. The room eventually began to fill up and soon nearly 100 people had assembled and the meeting began. I read my portion and listened as people began sharing about their lives and how they had managed to stay sober for a week. There was something special about this meeting; the people were happy and friendly. Through no fault of my own, I met some very special people there who remain friends with me to this day. During the meeting, while my mind worked on me, I began to get resentful--what a strange twist. And, of course, the resentment was over something extremely important. I realized that I was angry at the fact that the backyard at my house was overgrown with weeds, and there were tree branches that had been cut down, but not removed. How utterly insane. I was just released from prison, had spent three wonderful days playing with my two-year-old son, and now I was angry about weeds and branches in the backyard. This, of course, is common for newly sober people, and today I recognize that this sort of occurrence is actually quite common among my clan. We are, after all, quite a sick bunch.

At the end of the meeting, I brought the sheet back to the chairperson. As I walked up to the table where he was seated, he looked up at me and simply said "sit down." The amazing thing is that I did. A little guy, with curly, dark hair and black framed glasses, he was a real bookish looking sort. For me to obey his directive to sit down makes no sense to me, even today; but I did it. He looked over at me and asked me what was going on. I looked directly at him and told him that I had been released from the state penitentiary 72 hours ago. He didn't react; he simply said, "Ok, now I understand." Very deftly he removed a card from his wallet and wrote down a phone number on it; as he handed the card to me he told me, "Call me at 2:00 today, at that number." I stood up and told him that I would, and I left the meeting. I returned to Laura M's house and spent some time there with her and her husband talking about plans for the future and watching my boy play with her boys. After a while, I returned home, and for some reason, at 2:00, I called the guy from the meeting. His name was Roy; he was a math teacher at a local high school. I would run into him several years later when his school asked me to address the kids on substance abuse issues. He and I talked for a good long time while my son was napping. He seemed to understand why I was so angry and he helped me to put this situation into its proper perspective. I was truly amazed at how easy it was to talk with someone whom I had just met that morning, and even more amazed at how relieved I felt after talking with him. Oh yeah, and I solved the leaf and branch problem by making a game out of cleaning that stuff up with my son--how simple.

Karen returned that evening; we actually had a sweet reunion. Listening to her was wonderful, and helped me develop a sense of respect and admiration for her ability to survive while I was in prison. She is an amazing woman who did not deserve to be treated the way I treated her while I was fully in my addiction. We talked about my plans. In those first few days and weeks, I was able to develop the framework of a vision that included going back to school and learning how to take these awful experiences of addiction, disillusionment, incarceration, and now release and transform them into experiences that would somehow help others, and ultimately those I loved, and myself.

My first meeting with Jessie, my parole officer did not come close to what I expected it would be. Jessie was a very cool guy. I expected shame, reproach, and recrimination and what I got was acceptance, approval, and encouragement. He had obviously read the file and as we sat in his office at 19th Avenue and Camelback Roads in Phoenix, he expressed amazement at the fact that I had survived the prison experience. While I appreciated his recognition of that aspect of my situation, I was much more focused on what he wanted from me. What was he gonna make me do? I was totally ashamed of the whole specter of having to be supervised while living my life. I was all wrapped up in the false belief that I knew something about life and other stuff so why should I have to be monitored? I was also certain that he was gonna make me do demeaning stuff just to make an example out of me. As is often the case for me, it turned out very differently than I had imagined it would; Jessie only required some basic things from me. I was subject to urine drug screens on demand.

I had to attend group therapy with a man named Jake J., and I had to meet with Jessie once a month. I was completely taken aback by the simplicity of this prescribed program. He must have sensed this in me because what he said next had a profound impact on me. Jessie looked directly at me and said, "Hey look Hal, you are not a criminal." I was rocked to the very core of my soul. He continued, "I've seen criminals before and you aren't one. You fucked up, made some poor choices, and you have paid a very steep price for those choices. Now it's time to release yourself from the guilt and shame and make a life, and I will help you." I literally could not believe my ears, yet once again I wanted to believe that this was happening this way. I sat there and took it in as I stared at the floor. The tears came and that really pissed me off; here I was crying in the presence of my parole officer! After I gathered myself, I thanked him for his words and we went about finishing our meeting. I left there confused yet hopeful.

Those first few weeks were simply fabulous. I got to spend a lot of time with my son. We went everywhere together, including my job. At my parole hearing, my good friend Pete W. told the Parole Board that he would hire me immediately upon my release. He and John T. had created a business supplying Arabian horse farms with sawdust for the horse stalls. My job was to respond when the delivery came in, day or night, and to remove, as quickly as possible, all the 100 pound bags of sawdust from the semi-trailer; once that was done, I had to parcel out the orders and deliver them to the farms. I won't lie; it was hard work, but I was able to make some fun out of it by taking my son to see the horses and the trainers. Those horses actually live better than some people, and the trainers that I met were wonderfully patient with me. A number of them paid extra attention to my young son and encouraged him to interact with the horses. Being out of prison and having the luxury of interacting with my son and Arabian horses...I remain so very grateful for that time in my life.

I had also begun the process of healing relationships that I had destroyed through my own selfish, self-seeking addict behaviors. I began this process with my parents. They were so faithful to me throughout the entire ordeal. My mother never wavered in her belief that the police department was responsible for my being addicted to drugs. I think I helped her to understand that I had made the choices that led to me being locked up, but she was steadfast in her belief that the department could have responded differently. We had several talks about this and while she never relented on her perception of their accountability, I believe that she took some solace in the fact that I was able to reach a point of being accountable for the choices I made. It's still ironic to me that she and I were able to derive understanding from conversations we had in the visiting area of a state prison. This is confirmation for me that God's Hand is truly everywhere, and that the miracle of Grace, though sometimes difficult for us to conceive, is ultimately necessary to address addiction.

Now my father was quite a different story. Throughout the later years of his life he was still active in his use of alcohol, thus talk about my addiction to alcohol and drugs and the resultant personal accountability was difficult for him to abide. We were able to come to an understanding that I had made some really poor choices and needed to do what I needed to do.

I eventually met with the mayor of the City of Scottsdale, Herb D. I went right down to city hall and spent some time with him. He was a very special man, who welcomed me into his office and made no judgment about my past. After I told him that I was starting to figure out that I was most accountable in this scenario, he sat back in his chair, looked me directly in the eye, and told me that he was happy that I was out of that horrible place. He also said that he was glad that I had the attitude that I did and that he would do anything he could to help me. He also extracted a promise from me that I would not associate with any of the drug users from my past. I made a solemn oath in that office that day, and have lived up to that promise to this very day.

Next, I called the chief of police in Scottsdale, Fred C. The chief had been my sergeant when I first went to work at Scottsdale P.D. I met him for breakfast at Mag's Ham Bun in North Scottsdale. I faced the fear of meeting with him and it turned out to be a productive meeting for me. I told him that I was wrong in doing the things I had done, and I was willing to change, and needed to know from him what was necessary to right the wrong. This was all I could think of to say. I did ask him how I could square things between us. The chief told me to stay sober, and remember that some days would be better than others. I left that meeting feeling good about the process.

While I was attending 12-Step meetings I met a very nice man who ran a business out of the Air Park in North Scottsdale. We saw each other every morning because I was attending the 7:00 am meeting daily. He offered me a job delivering packages to his clients. Since my job with Pete did not have regular hours, this was perfect. I would see Jack at that meeting and he would let me know if had a delivery for me and where it needed to be delivered. I found myself going to hospitals all around the Phoenix area at least two or three times per week. He was paying me pretty good too, so I was happy and felt productive. The irony here is that I had no idea what was in the packages, so one day I asked. Jack explained that his business was a medical sterilization unit and they sterilized hospital instruments, including hypodermic syringes and that was the majority of what I was delivering!

One of the fondest memories I have is taking my young son Kevin with me to an Arabian horse ranch to deliver sawdust for the stalls. The ranch hands who I had come to know allowed Kevin and me to "pet" the horses. These large animals were very impressive to me, and the fact that my son was able to interact with them had a healing effect on me and provided a sense of bonding for my son and me. Life was very, very good for us in those precious moments.

I had told Pete that I was going to become a counselor for alcoholics and drug addicts. He supported me wholeheartedly in this process and shared with me that he only expected me to keep the job with him until I found a counseling gig. I scoured the papers every day for positions and went on several interviews.

The first one that I recall vividly was with a local inpatient rehabilitation center in Chandler, Arizona. I met with the director of the agency for an interview for a counselor technician position. This is a position similar to a recovery coach; it is for aspiring counselors who are not yet credentialed but have some experience in either actual recovery, or education, or both. I was excited that they wanted to interview me, so I put on a nice shirt and tie and arrived early for the interview. As I waited in the lobby, I saw patients of the facility and staff interacting and I was really excited about the prospect of working there. When the time came for the interview, I went in and met the director, who wanted a counseling professional with several years of experience in the management of people and the direction of programs. We talked about my application, and my relatively new recovery status. Now I had anticipated questions about my being convicted of felony narcotics charges and being imprisoned, but what happened next absolutely stunned me. The interviewer looked at me and told me that he had grave concerns about my ability to work with others. He told me that by reviewing my application he saw that I was a former police officer, and that I had been incarcerated for three years. I listened intently as he continued with his indictment of my past life. He told me that at this facility staff were required to treat people with kindness, understanding, and compassion, and he was concerned about how I would be able to do that given my past experiences. I responded by explaining that those very experiences, coupled with my learning to integrate the concepts of the 12 Steps into my life, were the bedrock of my ability to effectively interact with others in a safe, non-threatening, and nonjudgmental manner. He was not impressed or convinced. The interview was terminated and I was shown the way out with a half-hearted promise that he would call if he wanted to talk with me again.

I was reeling as I walked through the parking lot to my jeep. I was trying to make sense of what just happened, but those thoughts were overpowered by my sense of a need for immediate retribution. I was trying to figure out how I could go back there, blow the place up, not get caught, and make it home in time for supper.

I pulled into a convenience market just to stop and get my bearings. I threw a quarter into the pay phone and called my sponsor. Thank God. And thank God he answered. I told him what had just happened and he instructed me to "just breathe." I followed his instruction. I literally stood there with a phone in my ear just breathing. After several minutes, I calmed myself down and could talk again. Bill told me to come over to his house immediately. I got back into my truck and drove immediately to his house. The whole way over there I mulled the interview experience over in my mind, and here's the twist--on a conscious level I knew I was very angry...I just didn't know at what. Today it's obvious, but in that moment I had no clue.

When I got to Bill's house, he met me at the door, took me inside, gave me a nice cold soda, and led me out back onto the patio. I was in full anger mode, just ready to explode. He was so cool, actually placid. As we sat down he asked me what was going on in my mind; and what is really ironic is that I didn't know. Once we retraced that man's exact words to me--"We treat people with kindness, understanding, and compassion"--I saw that his concern about whether I would be able to do this may have been justified, given all that had occurred. This realization challenged my mind and my spirit to accept the possibility that I would not be able to treat people in such a fashion. Bill recognized this right away, and we were able to process this in such a way as to give my mind a rest, ultimately saving me and the clinical director from harm. It is ironic that his words evoked a series of thoughts and planned behaviors that would have actually proven him to be correct, when, in actuality, I was capable of dealing with the problems of others in an affirming, calming, and non-threatening manner. I am very thankful for the influence and insight of all those who were able to help me throughout this period of transition.

I would read the employment section of the paper every day looking for opportunities to get my foot in the door to do substance abuse counseling. One day, I discovered an advertisement for a counselor tech position with an agency called P.A.R.C. Place. The acronym was Phoenix Adolescent Recovery Center; I remember seeing the ad and immediately thinking "They will never hire me." Thank God I made the statement to my AA friend Bill as I was getting ready to make another delivery. In his West Virginia drawl, he made the comment, "Yeah, you're right, they won't hire you; and besides you have all those other prospects coming through your house every day and night." This, of course, brought me up short, and I resolved to at least go down there and fill out an application. I had all kinds of stuff going through my head on the way down there; I was torn between wanting to give it a try and knowing that nobody was going to hire the former cop, now felon. The noise in my head was deafening.

I went anyway. When I got there I said a prayer in the parking lot and walked into the lobby of this treatment center. This place was a converted nursing home and the receptionist was at the very front entrance. As I entered the reception area there were several people there, and the receptionist motioned for me to have a seat in one of the many oversized chairs in the vestibule. I sat down and watched as she deftly handled the people that were clamoring for her attention and service. My internal voice would not stop. "They aren't going to hire you; you are wasting your time and theirs; you don't have a chance." After several minutes of listening to this, I had had enough and got up to leave. This is when the miracle happened. The receptionist, in the middle of dealing with all the other people, somehow observed me rise and begin to leave. Without skipping a beat, she stopped dealing with the others, looked directly at me, and said "Here's the application you came for, and a pen, go right over to that desk, fill it out, and I'll be ready to take it from you once you're done." She said this in a voice tone that was very pleasant, yet that conveyed the expectation of compliance--that this wasn't a request. I complied. As I sat there filling in the required information I was amazed at how she would have known I was there for an application, and even more amazed at how she intuitively knew that I was struggling with whether or not I was going to go through with it.

I told my parole officer about applying for this job, and, as it turned out, he had worked with Patti C., one of the owners of P.A.R.C. Place, years before. I got an interview and don't remember much about it except that I told the clinical director that I didn't know if I would be a good counselor; I just wanted the opportunity to see if I could be. The director was really enthused about the fact that I was a former policeman. I also let him know about the felony conviction and, to my surprise, he was actually pleased about that, and most importantly that I was clean and sober. He told me later that having the felony conviction would give me credibility with the clients. At that interview I promised him two things: 1) I would show up on time every day, and 2) I would pass every drug/alcohol screen they gave me. I was then interviewed by Patti C; she was thrilled that Jessie M was my parole officer and she hired me at $7.50 an hour. I was ecstatic!! I was assigned to the temporary pool of counselor techs. I was required to call in every day to see if the census was large enough to warrant my being utilized each day. I could not have been happier!!! I was required to submit to a fingerprint check by the Department of Economic Security. They are a watchdog agency to ensure that youth are protected from child molesters, and others. I remember that when I went to get my fingerprints taken, I was asked if I had ever been convicted of a felony and when I answered affirmatively and was able to provide the examiner with the cause numbers and case identifiers he was amazed. Nearly a year later, I would be required to address the issue but initially there was no problem with the fact that I had been convicted of a felony.

I called the clinical director every morning at 8:31 am and asked "What time should I come in today?" I worked every shift he gave me, and after about a month of me calling him every day, he finally hired me on a full-time basis. I like to think that it had everything to do with my skills, abilities, and superior intellect. However, I believe it had more to do with the fact that I pestered him every day and to get some peace he hired me full time. We still joke about that today. He remains one of the best at dealing with adolescent life issues even today. We have remained friends and colleagues throughout all these years; I am very grateful for his grace and acceptance of me, as well as his willingness to take a chance on hiring the cop with the dubious past and uncertain future.

I learned a great deal working with the youth at PARC Place. The staff there was excellent as well. I met, or became reacquainted with, so many people during my eight years of working there. One of the first encounters was with Farrell. She was on staff there and once I got hired she told me that she had met me years earlier when I was a police officer. Apparently her husband had gone away on business and she was alone with the kids; something occurred at the home, some prowler or alarm call, and I was the one who responded. She regaled other staff members about how calming and professional I was in helping to settle her kids and her during that call. She was a great ally and teacher.

Terry was a primary therapist who had just completed her Master's Degree in social work at Arizona State University. She and I were talking one day and I told her that I was planning to secure an associate's degree in chemical dependency counseling from a local community college. Terry was able to extract from me that I was laboring under the belief that I was not smart enough to get a bachelor's degree. Watching her reaction was really funny; she stood all of about five feet four inches tall, and with a determination uncommon amongst most people, she literally herded me into her vehicle and took me over to ASU, where I first had an encounter with an automatic door that I tried to close and nearly broke. But we came away from that place with me signed up for the Bachelor's in Social Work program. Amazing how her spirit was able to overcome my negativity about my ability. I am so very grateful to Terry R for her ability to see in me what I was unable to see, and her willingness to mentor me.

I began attending classes at ASU. Admittedly in the first few weeks there I was convinced that any second someone was going to tap me on the shoulder and tell me that they made a mistake and I would not be allowed to continue. In retrospect, it is just astonishing how much fear I had about my past; I really do think that fear is the thief of all happiness in our lives. If nothing else, my completion of my college degrees taught me how to overcome the constant fear that I produced.

I am extremely loyal to the administration at Arizona State University. In my application to the School of Social Work, I told them in narrative form about my journey through prison and my desire to help others. In turn, they allowed me to attend classes there, and I know they didn't have to. I am so very grateful that they took a chance on me. I was one of the older students, and it was not long before my classmates and I interacted on several projects and people learned who I was, and where I had come from. I made many friends in that time and am grateful for their acceptance of me, and the opportunities being with those people afforded me. I was honored to be asked by my classmates to address the audience at our convocation ceremony. I was scared to death, but was able to give the speech without incident.

After one of my classes, the instructor asked to speak to me. I followed her to her office wondering what she wanted to talk with me about. She was a diminutive, yet very knowledgeable and assertive woman. Once we were in her office. she handed me a sheaf of papers and said: "You will go to graduate school young man... got it?" She was known for her use of the phrase "Got it." I looked at her and then at the papers and saw that she and several others had signed recommendations for me to attend the Master of Social Work program at ASU. I was astounded, grateful, and humbled. I applied for and was accepted to the MSW program at ASU and graduated with an MSW in 1996.

All the while I was attending school I was working at PARC Place. What an awesome opportunity to learn about human behavior, particularly those who were addicted, and the impact on families. Even as I write this I am reminded of recent contacts with people whose teenagers were in treatment with us; and there have been a few contacts from those young people who have now grown and become successful in their lives.

While there a couple of very poignant and impactful situations occurred that have left indelible marks upon me and my process of recovering a life out of the bondage of addiction. The first occurred within two weeks of my being hired at PARC Place. I had been befriended by two older women, Jeannie and Alice, who were both recovering alcoholics. Both adopted me and were like moms to me as I set about learning how to become an effective counselor. We had many late night sessions where these two kind souls spent hours simply being kind and tolerant by sharing their experience, strength, and hope with the former convict who so desperately wanted to find footing to make a life. Within two weeks, the medical director of the facility resigned to pursue other interests, and the new man happened to be the very same psychiatrist who had been assigned by the City of Scottsdale to evaluate me when I transitioned from being an undercover narcotics detective back to patrol. I had been a total jackass to this kind man by telling him that I didn't believe a word he said about wanting to help me, and I didn't really tell him anything but that. He tried his best to work with me but I was belligerent and simply a jackass. When I found out that he was coming to be the medical director of the very place I was now employed I was instantly thrust into fear, worry, self-loathing, and doom. This, of course, did not go unnoticed by my two "adopted moms," one of whom cornered me and with great care and understanding inquired as to why I was acting weird. I told her the situation and without missing a beat she helped me to see how this was a wonderful opportunity. Opportunity...opportunity for what? This was all my mind could scream at me--what kind of opportunity was this? When I finally got around to asking her she reminded me about my needing to clean up the wreckage of my past and to acknowledge that my behavior had been less than effective. I needed to face this man and mend the fence, as it were. Oh My God!!! Putting a recovery principle into action was just too much for me to think about--how gracious, tolerant, and loving were these two women. And after all my protestations and talking it out with them both, I came to the realization that they were 100% right and this was confirmed by my sponsor. I did the requisite writing and prepared for the process of making amends and accepting accountability for my past behavior.

On the day that the new director arrived I could hardly stand it. I wanted to get it over with but at the same time my mind made up all kinds of scenarios as to why this was a fool's errand and how many things would go wrong with this plan. Once I arrived at the facility and learned that the director was in his office, I said a quick prayer with Jeannie and then knocked on his office door. I remembered the voice as he asked me to enter and looked expectantly at me. It was clear that he did not recognize me; this fact later turned out to be key to my learning about this process. He didn't even recognize me, and still didn't after I told him my name. All this time I spent worrying about this, agonizing about what was going to happen, all the bad that my mind could conjure up, and the guy didn't even remember who I was. There is a great lesson in that for me.

He invited me to sit and I did. I looked over the desk at him and explained who I was and why I had asked to meet with him. His face began to change as he began to recognize and remember the situation. He listened intently as I explained to him that I had recognized that my behavior toward him had been horrible and I needed to be accountable for that. He sat back in his chair and looked me over for a few seconds and then his face brightened and he smiled directly at me. After a few minutes, he began to shake his head and began to remember more of the details of our interaction nearly four years past. He then said the most amazing thing to me, "Who could be better suited to help these kids learn about drugs?" I nearly fell off the chair. This was not the response I had expected.

He then asked how I was and we had a dialogue about the past four years. We talked for nearly a half an hour and then he realized that he and I both had work to do. We agreed to speak to one another often as he became more acquainted with the facility and staff and told me how glad he was that I had taken the time to speak with him. As I turned to walk out of the room he said, "Hal I want you to think about something, ok? I appreciate your making amends to me but I'd like you to think about who you really hurt, ok?" I was floored. I looked directly into his eyes and saw acceptance, forgiveness, grace, and acknowledgement of an attempt to right a wrong. I nodded, he smiled, and I left.

Of course, the second I left his office Jeannie grabbed me and wanted to know all the details. She smiled and wiped my sweaty eyes when I told her about how this kind and tolerant man had treated me respectfully and graciously when I had expected the worst. I learned so much that day and in the days that followed.

The second significant life event occurred nearly one year later. My work life was going great, I was going to college full time at Arizona State University, I was jumping through all the hoops that parole had set for me, and I was sober. But my marriage was in shambles. I believe out of shame and guilt I did not tell anyone, not even my sponsor, about the state of my marriage. This was a recipe for disaster. The thought that a good drunk would somehow make all this better began to slowly creep into my mind. The old adage about the monkey being off my back, but the circus is still in town, rang so true. But I put the volume down on that one and listened only to my own rationalization, justification, and minimization about why alcohol would solve this. Finally, I arrived at the breaking point on a Sunday morning after coming home late the night before from work to find that my wife was sleeping in the guest bedroom again, and I was alone.

When dawn broke on Sunday morning I had made up my mind to drink. My usual custom on Sundays was to get up early and walk to the store to buy the Sunday newspaper. As I was entering the parking lot of the convenience market a very large, brown, battered, and dusty car entered the same parking lot, and as I reached the parking curb, so did that vehicle. As the door to the vehicle swung open, my senses were assailed with the unmistakable odor of vomit, alcohol, urine, and feces all at once. I froze in my tracks on the curb by the ice machine as the female driver exited the vehicle and stopped to light a cigarette with shaking hands. Her dirty, scraggly hair was matted to her head, and her blouse and dress were covered with bodily fluids. I was dumbstruck. I walked to the door and she negotiated the curb, barely without falling, and shuffled toward the same door that I was moving toward. I held my breath and opened the door and waited as she threw the cigarette at the outside ashtray, and watched as she stumbled through the door I held open. Even with my breath being held the scent wafting around her was pungent and disgusting. I nearly lost the contents of my stomach. The clerk sized up the woman and looked directly at me as I let the glass door close. He gave me that knowing look of derision as he assessed the situation that was unfolding in front of him.

The woman mumbled that she wanted to buy some vodka. He, in his best customer service, condescending, and patronizing voice made it really clear to her that she would not be able to purchase alcohol for another couple of hours due to the law at the time. She settled for a pack of Marlboro Reds and pushed some money toward him. He haltingly accepted the money and produced a pack of cigarettes and she was soon teetering toward the door.

I had gone to the coffee pot and had prepared my coffee and retrieved the Sunday paper and moved to the other side of the counter to pay up. The clerk now had that disgusted, appalled yet exceedingly disdainful look about him as he completed my transaction. We did not share one word, but it was obvious to me how he felt about his encounter with this drunken woman. I made my way out of the store careful to hold my breath and avoid stepping in anything that had fallen from her during her trek in and out of the store. Once back in the parking lot, I watched as she attempted to light another cigarette while leaning heavily on the side of her car. With some difficulty, she got the smoke lit and got back into the vehicle, started it, and motored on out of the parking lot. She turned onto the street and was out of sight in a few seconds.

Of course, my mind was working on what I had just witnessed. It didn't take long for me to recognize that she was me if I chose to start drinking again. In that half mile back to my house I regained some personal perspective and decided that I would not drink for at least one more day. I had seen enough to convince myself that no matter how bad I thought things were going for me, drinking would only make matters worse.

Though very stark and indeed poignant, this would not be the end of this lesson. I got the brilliant idea to call my sponsor and relate my experience to him. He listened with bemused interest and asked if I wanted to hear his reaction to what I had told him. I certainly did and he started out with surprise at how things were at home for me. Funny how his phone hadn't rung prior to this was the way he put it!! Then he said "And not only that you don' know, do ya?" Of course I asked "Don't know what?" "You just don't know, do ya?" Don't know what for goodness sake??? Very deliberately he asked "You don't know that the second that car left your sight, that God didn't snap his fingers and bring her and her car back up to heaven." I was just overcome with awe at how he just knew that intuitively. He said that sometimes angels don't look angelic, but they are in our lives for a very real purpose; it appears that one of my angels showed up that day when God knew I needed her. Years later, my pastor and his wife would tell me about God's favor related to taking folks into their homes and the concept of Angels Unaware. That is recognizing that angels walk among us, and we are not always aware of their presence. Thank You God!!

I can recall coming in early on Saturday mornings and taking treatment kids from P.A.R.C. Place up to Papago Buttes to do their daily meditation and goal setting exercises. I was especially fond of the Wilderness Programs where we would take kids out for several days of being outdoors; initially, we would stay in cabins and plan activities such as hikes and other bonding exercises out in the woods. During these outdoor activities, I felt such a spiritual connection to

God; I constantly prayed offering my thanks and gratitude for having come from prison to these awesome experiences. I would often wonder who was treating whom? It is no wonder to me that I was able to augment my personal recovery from being in the situations presented to me by my work with these kids, their families, and the awesome staff I worked with. Years later, at a reunion, we all came together at a picnic in a Phoenix park. I cannot say enough about the lessons I learned from those wonderful, recovering people.

Terry is a very gifted therapist who adopted and mentored me. Terry, along with some others, also encouraged me to continue with my formal education all the while teaching me the nuances of working with young people with substance abuse and other issues. I recall Terry doing a specialty group with adolescent girls dealing with sexual abuse issues. Terry invited me to co-facilitate the group with her and I was immediately gratified and afraid at the same time. The fear came from not knowing how to relate to these abused young women; with Terry's expert guidance, we all learned how to effectively cope with issues that emerge as a result of life's path. Terry described me as a strong, yet sensitive male who was able to teach these special clients about appropriate boundaries and dealing with real world issues.

Mark Rhode, Curtis Walling, and Phil Lett, all psychologists, continually mentored me through this process of learning and relating to others. Each of these men encouraged me to continue with my education and learning and each employed me in some fashion; I am proud to say that I have working relationships with each of them today.

As time progressed and my training and experience increased, I was afforded the opportunity to serve in a variety of capacities. I interned, and actually supervised some staff members throughout my time at PARC Place. One of my fondest memories is when Frank Saverino came to work there. Frank was hired as a primary therapist, a position that I had applied for. Jim O., the clinical director, met with me and told me that while he was confident of my clinical abilities, I was just shy of obtaining my Master's Degree and he could not hire me for that job. I told him at that time that I needed him to watch me because I knew that I would be angry and resentful at the one he did hire. Well Jim hired Frank. And I tried my absolute best to be angry with him. Because of Frank's personality I just couldn't do it. We became very good friends and are still so to this day. In fact, Frank left PARC Place and hired me on at St. Luke's Behavioral Health Center, which led to my working as an employee assistance professional with police, firefighters, and other public safety personnel.

As I reflect upon those formative years after being released from prison I have a difficult time imagining any better place to have landed. I am eternally grateful to a compassionate, loving God who put me in the presence of such wonderful people to love, nurture, encourage, and trudge with me along the road of happy destiny.

Chapter 21

A MARRIAGE LOST
A LIFE SAVED

*M*y marriage was not flourishing. The wounds that I inflicted upon that relationship were too great for us to overcome. I was regularly attending 12-Step meetings, working the steps, yet it was hard for me to see recovery in our relationship. I recall one time attempting to make amends to my wife but she really was not interested. Not long after I got out of prison, we moved into a home that we rented and I had hoped to buy; in fact, we looked at many homes but never bought one. I was unable to see during this time that my wife had apparently decided that we were going to divorce and was struggling to figure out a way to tell me. Prior to learning this, I was doing all the right things and couldn't figure out why I was so unhappy. My wife had long since moved into one of the other bedrooms in our rented house, and it seemed like whenever I spoke to her she would not look me in the eye, and we rarely did anything together. As I continued to attend meetings, working the steps, and advancing my career, my marriage slipped further and further into the abyss.

December 17th, 1989, my son was turning three years old, and we wanted to have a birthday party for him. Friends and family were notified and preparations made; the plan was for us all to meet at a city park for a cookout and festivities. During this time in our lives, my wife and I were struggling in our marriage, and we weren't very effective in our communication with each other. Choosing a site for a celebration was a monumental task for us, given the dynamics of our relationship at the time. After several stops and starts we settled on Paradise Valley Park, which was several miles from where we lived. Little did I know that this simple choice would come to mean so much for my life and the lives of others.

The night before, as usual, I went to work at PARC Place. I worked until 11:00 pm, and was looking forward to seeing friends and celebrating the third birthday of my firstborn son the next day.

I awoke early on Sunday, and went to the park to reserve a ramada for the family and guests who we had invited. December mornings in Arizona are cold and crisp, so I dressed warmly. The sun was just starting to rise as I drove through the desert city in the frigid air watching in gratitude as I was blessed with a beautiful sunrise. Having been out of prison for a little less than a year, sunrises were a special treat. I stopped at a convenience market and got a large cup of coffee and the Sunday paper. The steam was rising from the cup as I went outside, got back into the car, and drove the few remaining blocks to the park.

I actually wondered if I had made the right decision about getting to the park so early. It was basically deserted. I even questioned the wisdom of the decision to have the party in this particular park, which was easily 15 miles from my home. Given the state of my marriage, having been recently released from prison, and on work furlough status, I found myself questioning everything I did. I was essentially without purpose; I had goals to become an alcohol/drug addiction counselor, but I had little confidence in my decisions. My whole demeanor was shame based and I felt like I was always doing things to make up for all the wrongs I had done. My life certainly had not gone as planned and many events had brought me to a point where my confidence was sorely wounded.

Even with all the self-doubt and self-recrimination I knew that a Power Greater than me had gotten me out of the self-imposed "bottom of the hole" to where I could, at least now, see daylight. I also had a notion that there was a deeper meaning underneath the events of the past three years, but I didn't know for sure what it was. I was just taking baby steps until I could eventually walk in the Sunlight of the Spirit again, although my thoughts weren't nearly as refined as these words indicate. Funny, I was actually unaware of these thoughts on a conscious level, yet I had an intuitive sense that some purpose was out there for me; I just didn't know what it was or how it was to be manifest. I also had hope that I would become well again, but for now I just struggled with even the most minor tasks and decisions.

As I waited in that park on that cold, crisp, clear December morning, reading the sports page and occasionally glancing up to see a bird fly by or perhaps a solitary coyote returning to its den after a morning hunt, I didn't see the other man enter the park behind me. This man moved purposely. He tipped over one of the large, gray, plastic garbage cans that were in the park, stood on the can, tied a rope around his neck, and slung the remaining rope over the branch of a nearby tree. He then stepped off the garbage can. The rope seized his neck like a vice grip. Most cunningly, it began to choke his life away leaving no room for change of heart. Only a deep, wrenching groan feebly moved passed the man's lips in one last grasp on life.

Two hundred yards away, I heard the groan and looked up from my paper. I heard the muffled cry and now began to look for its source. I saw the man all that distance away and questioned myself again. Was that a man hanging himself? How could that be? I ran toward the figure hanging from the tree and my only thought was if I could make it there in time?

When I reached the tree, the man appeared already dead. He was not breathing, no more groans of life, only silence. The world seemed to have gone quiet for one long second. No chirping birds, no wind, just silence from this place where a man had taken his life.

My mind was racing; I lifted the man to loosen the rope. I couldn't move the rope. This clothesline rope had embedded itself under his skin; it could not be moved. I cried out for help, "Somebody, anybody, please!!!" My fingers frantically searched for a way to loosen the rope. Another person arrived and together we worked to free the man from the rope. Finally, the rope surrendered its hold; the lifeless body fell into my arms and I laid him down on the ground.

I called upon my mind to remember my training. How do I start CPR? What do I do first? Can I help him? Is it too late? All these thoughts can confront a person when immediate action is necessary. In that brief instant, I shook off the doubts and felt my true strength. I could help this man. I knew what to do.

As we loosened the dead mans' clothing as he lay on the ground, I tilted his head back, pinched his nostrils, and began to breathe into him. I detected the unmistakably strong odor of alcohol on his breath. I continued to breathe in, and as my air escaped from his lungs, I prayed to God that he would live. I breathed over and over for what seemed like an eternity. Suddenly, a cough came from the dead man. I pulled back and saw this dead man open his eyes, utter a groan, and move jerkily to a sit-up position. He was alive! In what seemed like hours, but was only minutes, a man had died and was now alive.

A city park worker arrived at the scene and called the fire department. Upon their arrival, I briefed the paramedics on what I had seen and done. Still numbed by the impact of all that had just occurred, I left the area to return to the ramada I had reserved--the guests had begun to arrive for my son's birthday celebration.

As I slowly, almost reluctantly, left the scene, my mind began to reel. Emotions flooded my being. Could this be real? How had this happened? Why had I been there? Why was I chosen for this situation? Asking these questions of the God who knows all, I was quite simply overwhelmed with a flood of emotions that I still have difficulty describing.

I literally stood stock still one hundred yards away from the trauma scene, one hundred yards from friends and family gathering at the ramada--equidistant from both--I simply dropped to my knees, overwhelmed with gratitude. Tears began to flow freely from my eyes. In my conscious mind, I knew that God had now lifted a great burden from me. A kind, gracious, loving, and forgiving God had put me in position to be of help to another human being and, because I was sober, I had the ability to respond when called upon.

In my past life, I had been a police officer who in the course of duty shot and killed a man who was attempting to take my life. In that moment, I did not want to take another's life, however, with a gun pointed at me, my defense instinct came through. Everyday since I had found myself questioning if I had done the right thing. That scene played over and over in my mind daily. How could I have handled it differently?

Since that day my life had taken a downward spiral. I had used drugs and become addicted while working as an undercover narcotics detective before the shooting. Although I was clean and at the time of the shooting, the follow-up investigation brought to light my addiction to drugs and criminal offenses associated with that addiction; I had been imprisoned and had served nearly three years of a seven-year prison sentence and, while I was on parole status, God set up this meeting.

Six months after my release from prison I was in a park. I thought I was there to celebrate the birthday of my son and maybe that was part of it, but now I believed there was a higher purpose. In his infinite wisdom, God used a man who had lived through the shame, guilt, and remorse of addiction to drugs and alcohol, the trauma of taking another man's life in defense of his own, and the even stigma of prison, to preserve the life of a misdirected and perhaps tortured soul.

I cried uncontrollably for several minutes. I was alone, on the ground, prostrate before my God and unable to fully grasp all that happened, yet knowing something had changed in me and the way I was to look at my life and the lives of others.

Eventually, I composed myself enough to stand and traverse the ground between where I had fallen and the ramada where my family and friends had gathered. What was happening? Is he

also told me that he was so happy that I was no longer in prison. I was puzzled by this degree of elation and he sensed it. Without me asking, he told me that he and others had followed the accounts of my case and were all saddened when the facts dictated that the judge had to send me to prison. This man was clearly telling me the truth and it served to accelerate the healing process in me. He told me he was there to bring attention to this situation to the media. My reaction was visceral. I was instantly terrified. I had experience with media in the not-so-distant past, and it was not good. The lieutenant sensed my trepidation and asked me what I was thinking. I told him that I would appreciate his not alerting them to our being here at the park because I did not want to expose my family and guests, nor myself, to them. He understood completely and told me that he would alert them in the normal fashion and that he would have positive things to say about what had happened that day. Moreover, he told me that he would be recommending to the chief of police that I be recognized with a Life Saving Award. I was truly humbled in that moment. I was also more than a little afraid of what all that attention might bring.

The next morning an article appeared in the *Arizona Republic*. There was mention of a man's life being saved and I was credited with doing that. That Monday morning I was in a class at Rio Salado Community College. Several of my colleagues brought the newspaper article to class with them and they all had a fabulous time razzing me about not being able to stay out of the media.

True to his word, the lieutenant made the recommendation to the chief of police and about a month later my family and I were invited to the Desert Horizon Precinct for the award ceremony. My wife, my son, and I went and were greeted by the precinct commander and others. A proclamation was read, plaques were given to me and the other person who had helped, pictures were taken, and I recall my son and I eating cake! What a day it was.

I was also provided with contact information for the young man and his family. We had several telephone conversations throughout the years but he would never come to meet me and we eventually lost contact with each other. I am truly grateful to all who were a part of that day; I remain convinced that God provided an opportunity for healing and transformation on that day in a park where perhaps two lives were saved!

Life on life's terms continued on for me. While many positive things were happening in different spheres of my life, I was unable to see during this time that my wife had apparently decided that we were going to divorce and was struggling to figure out a way to tell me. We began marital counseling because I saw that as a way to perhaps overcome the mistakes I had made in that relationship. My wife told the counselor that we would be divorcing; the counselor would not tell me, but told my wife that she needed to tell me. She struggled with this and eventually told me by telephone. As I write this, I am reminded that the disease of addiction not only affects the addicted. Through the addicted person it also destroys sweet relationships in a sometimes slow, and painfully agonizing grip as it depletes souls of grace, love, and eventually life.

In the days immediately following Karen telling me that we would be divorcing, I was plunged into extreme shame, guilt, fear, and remorse. I knew that my behavior had caused this, and I didn't know how to deal with that. I recall driving places and having to pull the truck over to the side of the road and cry. I knew that the relationship with Karen was over. No one deserves to be treated the way I treated her. My selfish, self-centered thinking and behavior were atrocious and I don't blame her one bit for leaving. However, in those moments when it became a reality, I was angry and fearful that I would never see Kevin again. Thankfully, God has seen fit that Kevin and I would have a significant relationship.

Chapter 22

MY SOULMATE

In the aftermath of my divorce from Karen I focused on staying sober and completing my formal education. Things were going well at work. While I was so afraid that I wouldn't see Kevin, I actually felt a sense of relief that my relationship with Karen was at least clarified.

My best friend and AA sponsor, Bill S., was a near constant companion, and he introduced me to some wonderful people, including his family, and friends he had made throughout the years. One such friend was a truck driver named Dave. Dave actually rented his home to Karen and me and remained my friend when I had to move out after the divorce. There came a time in 1991 when Dave chose to be married. The ceremony was to take place in the tranquil setting of our mutual friend Bill's backyard. As the date approached, I recall being in therapy and during our sessions we would talk about my taking a date to this wedding; to that end, I had asked approximately ten women out to this event and each, for various reasons. turned me down. I was actually beginning to wonder if there was something wrong with me. Several of my friends were all too quick to point out that there were several things wrong with me. At any rate, since I was having no success securing a date for this wedding, I made the decision to have my young son Kevin accompany me.

On the day of the wedding, I arrived early, as is my custom. The house and yard were decorated appropriately and, after greeting my friend and entering the backyard, I was immediately drawn to a young woman who was there early as well. I learned she had been asked to sing for the ceremony. Quite simply she was, and still is, the most gorgeous creature I have ever seen! Framed beneath the flowered arch, in the afternoon sun in that backyard, she took my breath away. I was instantly attracted to her and, at the same time, "knew" instantly that she would never be available. I mean, how could such a beautiful woman be single? And even if by some miracle she was single, what could she possibly want with me? All of these thoughts occurred at lightning speed while I stood in that backyard that fateful day.

I immediately sought out my friend Bill to inquire about this beauty and much to my surprise learned that she was single, and actually had no current beau. I was also informed by my friend that if my attitude and behavior were appropriate, he would introduce me to this woman, whose name was Ellen.

What my good friend didn't tell me was nothing short of the stuff that dreams are made of. At the rehearsal dinner the night before the ceremony, all the participants were gathered, including Ellen. Now it seems that Ellen had been in several romantic relationships, but had never married and was given to believe that she would not ever marry; she had read in a magazine that the way to find a suitable mate is to let people in your social network know that you are looking, and the type of person you are looking for. The theory goes that your supporters would then provide you with leads of those who fall within the criteria you shared. As it turns out, Ellen decided to test this theory at the rehearsal dinner and told my friend Bill, and his wife, Ann, the type of person she was looking for. As it turns out, Bill was the father of Ellen's best friend, Mary, and Ellen had been a regular in Bill and Ann's home throughout her teen years. So as Ellen is telling Bill and Ann that she is looking for a man with a strong resolve, yet a sense of humor, and appropriate sensitivities, both Bill and Ann remark that such a man, Hal, would be attending the wedding the next day. Each suggested that Ellen check him out. Now do you think either of them told me this--no, they just let the natural and logical consequences occur.

As the wedding ceremony concluded and the dinner began that evening, it was nothing short of magical. As the story is told by Ellen, now my wife, she had been watching me and had gotten into the serving line near me and Kevin. She observed how we retrieved sodas from the coolers and how the cooler lid fell on Kevin's hand and how he started to cry in pain. Thinking quickly, I reached out with my foot and kicked the cooler saying, "Bad cooler." This evoked the same response from the little boy, who stopped crying as we kicked the cooler together. Ellen would later say that this humorous sight of an alleged adult and a child kicking a cooler was instrumental in beginning the relationship we enjoy today. As we made our way to a table in that comfortable backyard setting, Ellen joined us for supper and I found it difficult to speak while gazing upon her awesome and stunning beauty. I was literally mesmerized by those dazzling blue eyes, and for one of the first times in my life I was at a loss for words. It is an absolute wonder that we ever got to know one another because I was completely awestruck by her physical beauty, and by the gentle tone of her voice, softness of her face, and the ease and comfort when she smiled or laughed--pure magic this is.

We spoke by phone several times after that and I came to realize just how regimented my life was. Working full time in an adolescent treatment center, going to school full time, single parenting commitments, and working an active recovery program does not leave a lot of time for dating. It would be several months before we actually saw one another again, and, as it turned out, it was well worth the wait.

At Christmastime, I was invited over to my friend Bill's house, where, as was Bill and Ann's custom, they had gathered together friends and family in the living room, around the Christmas tree, to sing Christmas carols. Now this was new to me; I don't sing. I was a former Marine, former cop, and out of prison on Parole; if my friends could see me singing Christmas carols with a group of real people--amazing stuff. So while I'm wondering how in the heck I had gotten there, I heard a knock on the door and who should be there but Ellen. All the guests who had been seated around the living room rose to greet her at the front door, including me. What happened next is very cool! After greeting her at the door, we all turned back to our seats. Wouldn't you know it, as it turned out, there was only one place for her to sit--right next to me. As the evening progressed, I found myself turning to her and asking if I could get her a drink, or something to eat. It was magical. I have a habit, even to this day, of carrying a pen clipped to the opening of my shirt. I think I developed this habit as a police officer. Anyway, on this night, I had apparently clipped the pen to my shirt and it leaked. Ellen noticed this and while we were standing in the kitchen reached out with her hand and touched me where the pen had leaked. I thought I would fall over. She touched me....she touched me!!!

I managed to get her work phone number that night and I called her each day for three straight days with no answer. She had taken some time off for the Christmas break. It was excruciating waiting to get to talk with her. On the third day, when I reached her, I made a date to go to her dog grooming shop to see her. I spent almost three hours there talking with her as she groomed dogs and talked with co-workers and customers. I felt so comfortable talking with her, I asked her out on a date. She agreed and so we went out to a nice Italian restaurant in Phoenix that eventually became "our restaurant" until it closed up several years later. After dinner, we saw *Russia House*, the most boring movie ever made. I didn't care; I was with "Her." Ellen had become "Her." I was in love like I had never been in all my life.

We went out on New Year's Eve to a sober friend's house and played pinochle and celebrated the New Year. We talked about so many things in such a short period of time. I told her all about my past and how committed I was to sobriety. I also told her about how committed I was to helping others overcome addiction and other issues in their lives. After some time, I introduced her to Kevin; we all went to the zoo together. Forever etched upon my mind is the sight of Ellen and Kevin holding hands and walking and talking together while I went in search of refreshments. Ellen had told me how important it was for her to have a relationship with Kevin, but for him to know that she was not going to replace his mother. What absolutely incredible insight!! Another moment of insight was not so easily resolved. I learned that parenting a little boy was different when a woman was actively involved. This became apparent when we all three went out to get a movie to watch. action adventure movies were Kevin's and my favorites so you can imagine our shock when she informed us that we would not be watching R rated or even PG-13 movies with her. I will never forget looking into his eyes and realizing that our lives were changing...and for the better!!!

I surprised her with a wedding ring the next Christmas; we were married the following spring. As of this writing, we have spent 22 years together. While we have disagreements now and then our married life has been relatively free of contention and strife. Early on, I had taken notice of the fact that when we were out on dates Ellen would not drink alcohol. I knew that she was a casual drinker from conversations that we had, and from others in our social network. One day, I asked her about it and she said that she was not drinking around me out of respect for my choice of not drinking. I told her that I appreciated her support but there were issues I had with *her* not drinking out of deference to me. First, I was afraid that she would eventually become resentful about not being able to drink in situations where she would normally drink; and secondly, if she drank alcohol in an abusive or dependent manner then we needed to know that to advance the relationship. She was appreciative of the frankness of our conversation and on our next date when the server asked she ordered a margarita. Now this was fascinating because I watched her take this drink and play with the straw and stir it. I mean she nursed this drink for at least a half an hour and didn't even drink it all. When the server asked if she was done I nearly fell off my chair when she said "yes," and then refused another one and ordered an iced tea instead!! I was completely floored; in fact, I had to process it with her later because I had never in my lifetime seen anyone able to do that. She matter-of-factly told me that this sort of thing happens all the time so get over it! I am happy to write that Ellen has never stood between me and going to AA meetings, or any other activity that supports my not drinking. Throughout the years, she and the kids have made the yearly trek to my home group and watched as I collected a yearly chip commemorating another year of sobriety. She and they are blessings in my life.

Life was a daring, bold adventure for Ellen and me in the beginning. I was going to college full time and working full time so when we threw in together we had to adjust to all that was happening in our lives. Ellen also began school and she had her own dog grooming shop that demanded a great deal of her time. When I graduated with my Bachelor's Degree from ASU, I was so very proud. I had overcome a great deal just to get that far, and perhaps the most significant obstacle to have overcome was the mistaken belief that I was not worthy enough to attend such a prestigious school. One of the proudest moments of my life came when the leaders of our small social work class came and asked that I address the class, families, instructors, and guests at the social work graduation ceremony. I was a nervous wreck! I got through it with Ellen's help. I can see the faces of all my family, friends, and colleagues in the crowd, but mostly I see that beautiful wife, mother, and friend.

Almost immediately after completing my Bachelor's Degree, I was accepted to graduate school at Arizona State University. I am truly indebted to that institution for their grace and belief in me. From the beginning, going to advanced classes proved to be a challenge for me. Academically, the material was arduous and I nearly quit after beginning the first course--those old demons returned and I began to believe that I was not able to comprehend the material. A talk with the instructor helped me with that issue and I continued on. Most memorable are the nights I would return from having worked all day, now at St. Luke's Behavioral Health Center, and having attended a three-hour class. I would pull into the driveway of our modest home, and Ellen would meet me at the carport door as I uttered the words "I'm quitting school." She would smile and welcome me into the house and listen to my whining and we would resolve that I would quit next week. She was so very patient.

I knew that I wanted to earn the Master's Degree, but I missed being with her and my second son, Collin. Thank you God for the perseverance to continue on in those moments when I didn't want to. Thankfully, the days turned into weeks, the weeks into months, and the months into years, and I was done!! We had a big party at the house, my parents took us out to dinner at the Spaghetti Company, and I graduated with a Master's Degree in Social Work in 1996!! I felt so very proud about this accomplishment, and still do today.

Collin Samuel Johnson Nevitt was born on March 13th, 1994, and Mariah Rose Nevitt was born on February 1st, 1998. Collin is now a sophomore at Arizona State University, where he earned an academic scholarship. Throughout his high school experience, Collin was a captain of his wrestling team, and in his senior year was named Most Valuable Wrestler for his team.

Mariah Rose is a sophomore in high school. She enjoys acting in plays for various groups in the Phoenix area, and presently has earned the lead role in *Fiddler on the Roof.*

It has been a challenge raising these wonderful children. They each have distinct personalities and behaviors. I marvel at how Collin and Mariah have bonded with my oldest son Kevin and his family. Kevin enjoys skydiving and is training to be an instructor.

This story would not be complete without "The Thanksgiving Story." On our third Thanksgiving Day together after we were married Kevin got to spend the night with us on Wednesday. He was going to be with us throughout the whole weekend. On Thanksgiving morning, once we all got up, Ellen chased the boys--Kevin, who was nine years old; Collin, who was then three years old; and me, at approximately 40 years old, out of the house so she could get the turkey prepared. Apparently we were in the way. So we decided to take Rocky the boxer dog to the park a couple of blocks away from the house.

Once we had walked to the park, I noticed that it was cold enough and early enough in the day that there was a layer of frost still on the grass. As the three boys and the dog walked through the park, the frost crunched under our feet as we trudged along.

About a third of the way through the 200-yard-long park, we found a large, empty, cardboard box lying innocently enough on the grass. Almost instantly the idea came to me that it would be cool if we could put Collin in the box and have Rocky pull him on top of the frosted grass. Collin and Kevin both thought it would be fun--what could go wrong?

So we all took our positions. Collin was in the box holding tightly to the leash attached to the collar on Rocky's neck. When I said "Sit Rocky," he obliged and Kevin and I then positioned ourselves some 25 yards away. "You ready Collin?" "Yeah dad" came the reply. "Rocky come!"

Instantly the 85-pound dog sprang from sitting to running full speed toward Kevin and me. The leash grew taunt as Collin tried his best to hang onto it. The leash ripped out of his hands and the dog sprinted to where we were waiting while the box and the boy did not move an inch.

We brought the dog back to the box and the boy and tried to figure out how to make this happen. I told Collin to hold his leg up. He put his small leg up toward me and I then looped the leash over his foot. We were all smiles as we simultaneously pictured what was now going to happen. Kevin and I repositioned ourselves 25 yards away again. "Rocky sit. Ready Collin?" "Yep, ready dad." "Rocky come!"

Once again the big dog sprang into motion. Collin's leg held the leash and the box began to slide along the frosted grass. Squeals of delight came from Collin. Kevin and I were laughing as the dog, box, and boy made their way toward us. That's when things got interesting!!

I moved to my right and began moving the opposite direction that the boy, box, and dog were moving. My intent was that Rocky would follow me and we would keep the ride going. Rocky didn't follow me. Instead he came to a stop and rather than follow me he leaped straight back over Collin and then started to follow me. Well, the leash followed, and the leg attached to the leash followed, as did the boy attached to the leg. First the leg went straight up in the air and as the leash grew taut again the boy was removed from the box.

Now both I and Kevin are running and laughing. Collin is laughing as he is being dragged along the frosted grass. Essentially, he is plowing up the ground as he rolls from side to side behind the sprinting dog. After several steps, I figured out that if I stopped running Rocky would stop. So, while laughing uncontrollably, I dropped to my knees and the dog quickly made his way to where Kevin and I were stopped.

We were all laughing. Rocky went from Kevin, to Collin, and me licking our faces and wagging his tail. Collin was filthy. He was literally covered from head to toe with dirt and grass. Kevin finally asked, "What are we gonna tell Ellen?" At this I began brushing the dirt and grass off of Collin and I told them in my best parental voice, "It's probably best that I tell Ellen." They both agreed. As we walked toward the house, we continued to recount this adventure, laughing and remembering different aspects of the occurrence.

As we walked up through the driveway of our home I could see Ellen in the kitchen. She met us at the back door. Instantly, she observed Collin's condition, and demanded to know how her son had gotten so dirty. The boys both looked at me as I gulped and said "Well, he was never in any danger." "What did you do to that boy?" she demanded. As I told the tale of our adventure, her incredulous tones of "You did what?" and "What were you thinking?" echoed through our home. It didn't help that the boys were laughing and nodding as I tried my best to explain my thought process for this grand adventure to a woman who had absolutely no sense of humor or sense of boyish adventure in the moment. Eventually, she forgave my faulty thinking and thankfully thought better of calling Child Protective Services. This has become one of our favorite Thanksgiving stories.

After some time, I got up enough courage to face the judge who had sentenced me to prison. I recall making the telephone call to his office requesting to speak with the judge. When his secretary asked who I was and I told her, the silence on the other end of the phone was deafening. I assured her that the judge had nothing to worry about from me, that I was calling in peace. She was hesitant but told me to wait on the line. In a few minutes, the judge came on and I told him that I wanted to meet with him for the purpose of "mending fences." I really did not know what this term actually meant, but I heard that Dr. Bob Smith, one of the original founders of Alcoholics Anonymous, was fond of this term as it related to making amends for past wrongs. To my utter amazement, the judge accepted my invitation, and, as it turned out, had to be in the jury room of the Superior Court later that week because he had been selected for jury duty, and had to complete paperwork to be excused from that assignment.

On my way to that meeting, I realized that we had unintentionally scheduled the meeting for June 28, 1993, exactly seven years to the day after he had sentenced me to seven years in the Arizona State Penitentiary. My emotions were running high as I sought him out and found him in the crowded room at the Superior Court building in downtown Phoenix. As we settled into the plastic chairs and he worked on his paperwork to be excused from jury duty, we shared a laugh about that. I was excited, afraid, and eager all at once. He was gracious, calm, and curious about this meeting. I told him that I had been out of prison for three and one-half years and that I was studying at Arizona State University, and working full time in the addiction treatment field. The judge was encouraging and told me that he always knew that I was "A winner." I was amazed that he would say that, and even more amazed that he appeared to genuinely believe that. I told him that I had been working in the addictions field for more than three years. I then told him that I was there to make amends for my behavior, and that I was fully convinced that I had placed him in a bad position by forcing him to sentence me to a prison term. I had had ample time to think about this, so I told him that I was initially angry with him, but had come around to a different way of thinking as time went on. I recall that he nodded his head a lot and looked directly at me during the entire time I was speaking to him, but I had no idea what he was thinking.

I told him that in my work with teen drug addicts and their families I had experienced a lot of satisfaction, and the people I worked for had given me the opportunity to learn more about addictions and the process of helping, and had encouraged me to stretch my professional abilities. I shared with him that I had even been placed in a supervisory capacity and that one of the folks I was supervising had been assigned as a correctional officer at the prison where I had been housed. I ended with recognizing that it was his ability to exercise spiritual courage in sentencing me that led directly to changes in my thinking and behavior, and it was that initial choice that had resulted in positive changes in my life, and the lives of several others. At that point, I thanked him for making the choice of sending me to prison, and acknowledged that while initially painful, and not something I would recommend to others, his choice was the right thing for me, for the community, and for the criminal justice system.

The judge was silent. It seemed like he didn't speak for several minutes as he let my words sink in. I didn't know what to do so I just stared at him while he took it all in. When he finally spoke he looked right at me and told me that he was at a loss for what to say. He laughed and said that he was certain that in his career as a judge never had a defendant thanked him for sentencing them to prison. He also said that he appreciated the fact that I was able to make the change in thinking about accountability for my behavior. He invited me to walk with him from the jury room, so we left and went up on the elevator to the floor where his courtroom was located. We talked about the aftermath of the shooting trial, and the comment I had made to the press about going back to my life "such as it is." He said that he remembered that. I recall that he introduced me to several other people who were walking past us. I don't remember who they were; I just remember how surreal I thought this whole time was. I mean here I was conversing with the very man who had sentenced me to prison--only a purposeful, merciful, kind, loving, and faithful God could dream this up!! The judge and I shook hands and parted ways; he did ask if he could call me later, and he did. We talked by phone on one occasion after that and I didn't see the judge again until 13 years later when he and his wife visited my home.

In June 2006, I celebrated 20 years of continuous sobriety. My wife and some of my friends arranged for a party at my home. Guests included several of my recovering friends from differing fellowships, people whom I worked with from the State Bar of Arizona, and other folks I had met along the way. Included in those invited was Judge Ted N., my sentencing judge, who had actually retired from the Arizona Court of Appeals several years earlier. It was with utter amazement that I looked across my living room and observed the judge and his wife conversing with a group of lawyers from the State Bar of Arizona, all with whom I worked with at the time. What's more, as I listened to the conversation, one of them thanked the judge for his handling of my case. Recovery birthdays are heady stuff, but this was just way off the charts as far as I was concerned; again, it was all part of God's plan and at times difficult for my human brain to grasp. Anyway, as I watched this unfold, the judge looked over at me and motioned me to come over to where this gathering was. Now it's my living room, but he's the judge, so I obediently went over to where he was standing with the others. He shook my hand and said "congratulations, this is a very special day for you." I responded with a "Yes it is and thank you, and thank you for coming here." He told me that this was a special day for him as well. I didn't know what he was referring to so I asked him what he meant. Now it's important to note that the judge is a former Marine, and he knew that I was as well. He looked directly at me and said "Well look around you knucklehead...what do you see?" I looked around at a houseful of guests all in various conversations with each other. I became aware of the ease and comfort they were experiencing, the laughter, the communication, and the kids in attendance as they ran and played--just the simplicity of a group of people in celebration of an accomplishment by someone they knew. When I turned back to him and described what I saw, he said something that absolutely blew me away. "I never get to see this" is what he said. In that moment, as we locked eyes, I began to understand that this man had sentenced numerous people to prison and that was the last he had seen of them. I was rocked to the core of my being. What a powerful realization. I was humbled, and then briefly I got all puffed up thinking that I was about something again. The judge sensed this and very quickly brought me right back to reality. He said "Hey before you go getting all full of yourself, hear this--whatever you're doing, keep doing it; and if you stop I'll find out about it." I have never forgotten those words.

Some years later I was fortunate enough to be afforded the opportunity to be an assistant coach on my son Collin's Pop Warner football team. At the beginning of that process I was required to fill out a background check form. Now, of course, I was anxious about this even though I had disclosed my past to the head coach. So after filling out the form, I was busy being nervous at practice and the coach approached me and asked what was going on with me. I told him that I was worried about the background check, so he took me aside and explained the following to me. Every year the kids are required to have two hours of "Don't Do Drugs" education through the team. The coach went on to explain that every year he got up in front of the kids and gave them a lecture about not doing drugs. He explained further that it was very awkward for him to do this since he had no experience, and the talk was usually boring and consisted of him simply droning on about this subject while the kids ignored him. He looked directly into my eyes and said "Now I don't have to do that this year, do I?"

I was stunned. His face lit up, and mine did too. For the next two years on cool, crisp, fall evenings I was given the opportunity to tell a group of kids, coaches, parents, and others about my experience, strength, and hope as it pertained to drug addiction and recovery. And, on one of those fall evenings, we heard from a judge. The very judge who had sentenced me agreed to address those kids, coaches, and parents about his experience with the former policeman whom he had sentenced to prison and who now was using his experience to benefit others. When I think of all that God has done in my life I am truly amazed at the situations that have emerged after the miracle of healing has occurred.

Ellen, the kids, and I are actively involved in church ministries at Oasis Community Church in Scottsdale, Arizona. Ellen is a worship leader, using her vocal talent to serve the church and community. I was challenged by my pastor several years ago to serve in the recovery field, so with the help and support of several others in the church we have regular recovery meetings to meet the needs of people in the church with addiction issues. The kids attend youth activities, are involved in drama outreach, and other service-related activities in the church.

Several years ago, Ellen and I collaborated to form a company, Innovative Workplace Solutions. It is a consulting organization that utilizes her talents as a human resources professional, and my talents as a mental health provider to serve client companies with needs for those services. Through this company we have had the good fortune to collaborate on service provision to others through mediations, trainings, and other professional activities. We both agree that we are learning from each other in our working together and believe that we have had positive impacts on those to whom we have provided services.

Today we enjoy a relationship based on love and respect for one another. We have raised our children to be respectful of others and they are active, intelligent, and leaders in their respective peer groups. Thank You God for this woman's role in my life!

Chapter 23

GRACE AND GOD'S

*W*e sold our home in central Phoenix in 1997 and moved to a quiet, middle class neighborhood in northeast Phoenix. We found a school for Collin and Mariah and began settling into our new surroundings. Over the next few years we found restaurants to enjoy, hiking trails to conquer, and other aspects of establishing our lives together.

Part of the settling into the new community process was Ellen finding a church for the kids to attend. God has such perfect timing, and a great sense of humor as evidenced by what happened in this process.

As my life has unfolded, my relationship with God/Christ has changed. For a great deal of time I ran from God. I was convinced that God wanted to punish me for all my past sins. I just knew that God had been keeping score and he was really pissed off at me for being so weak, and was further annoyed at my willingness to engage in all manner of riotous living, all the way from drug and alcohol abuse, stealing, lying, cheating, and not going to church!!

All of this changed when I got arrested in 1986. How quickly I reverted back to prayer, particularly that prayer that a lot of us have prayed: "If you get me out of this I'll never do that again"; or _____ (you fill in the blank). The whole situation of being addicted, arrested, convicted, and imprisoned helped to get me closer to God. While I was in prison I developed the habit of daily prayer, and my working through the steps of the 12-Step program helped to alter my conception of God and my relationship with Him.

However, it wasn't until I was married to Ellen I came to a deeper, more meaningful understanding of the concept of Grace and God's never ending love for me. I had been attending 12-Step meetings regularly; was sober, employed, and raising kids; and I believed that my life was progressing nicely. Ellen approached me one day and told me that she thought it a good idea for the kids to go to church; alarm bells started going off in my head!! I listened with some fear about what she expected of me, and, as it turned out, she really didn't expect much, just to support her in the idea that she would be taking the kids to church. Whew! OK, no problem.

So one Sunday morning they go off to church and I stay home and watch football. The next week, as they are preparing to leave, my son, Collin, in his five-year-old way, tells Ellen that he doesn't want to go to church but wants to stay home with dad--alarm bells again!!

The conversation went something like this: "Now Collin, don't you want to go to church to thank God for all our blessings like our house, our food, and other stuff?" And of course Collin retorts with "Well I did that last week mom." After going round and round like this for a while Ellen looked at me with that exasperated look and I knew she wanted me to help with this situation. As a five-year-old, Collin was very good when it came to making choices, so I presented him with the following scenario: "Collin you gotta go to church but you have a choice." He asks "Ok, what's the choice?" I tell him, "Well you can go to church and have fun playing with the kids like you did last week or you can go over there and have no fun at all, and I suggest you go and have no fun." After several seconds of deep contemplation he responds with "No way...I'm gonna go have fun!" And with that he runs to the waiting car to go to church. Ellen is ecstatic, throws her arms around me, gathers up her stuff, and off they go.

Of course, I feel good about my wonderful parenting skills until I observe the taillights of Ellen's car go out of sight. The thought suddenly came to me that I had set up the very same scenario that my parents had set for me when I was my son's age. I know now that this was the Holy Spirit convicting me. When Ellen and the kids returned I sat down with her and rather sheepishly confessed my new found knowledge and understanding of the dynamic I had just created. As we talked this through I made the decision to begin attending church again. Yeah, I was gonna give the God of the Universe one more chance. I know now how utterly ridiculous my thinking had actually become. Now I hadn't stepped foot in a church since the mid 1970s, so the following Sunday, as I was preparing to go to church with my family, I was putting on a necktie when my wife informed me that it was highly unlikely that anyone else would be wearing a necktie. "Not even the Pastor?" I asked incredulously. "Well maybe the Pastor," was her reply. I wore the necktie anyway.

So it was off to church we went as a family. Was I ever in for a big surprise!! Ellen had been right. Nobody was wearing a tie but me. There was an actual band that played loud worship music and the pastor skipped the hell, fire, and brimstone stuff and made references to real life issues that I could relate to. In fact, he actually mentioned the need for substance abusers to attend 12-step meetings. The people in attendance were real people. They were in large part casually dressed people, but nonetheless real people, the majority of whom seemed happy, joyous, and free. I was instantly drawn to this group and began regular attendance at Friendship Community Church.

That church has seen many changes over the years. Ellen is now one of the worship leaders and is actively involved in delivering the message of the never-ending love of Christ through music, skits, and other venues. The church merged with another church and has now become Oasis Community Church, and as a church body we are actively engaged in reaching out to the community to spread the good news of salvation, forgiveness, grace, redemption, and service to others.

The result of this attendance at church has been nothing short of miraculous to me. I NEVER envisioned joining a church. I joined. I NEVER envisioned being part of a pastoral search team. I was appointed to the team. I NEVER envisioned doing an outreach ministry for street children and others in another country. My son Collin and I went to Mexico where God used my Spanish speaking skill to minister to kids on the street. I NEVER envisioned being asked to lead a recovery ministry. I was asked to lead such a ministry.

As I learned more about salvation and the life of Jesus Christ I became aware that I had yet to be baptized. On a beautiful Sunday afternoon after the church service, my wife and youngest children observed their husband and father following the command of our Lord to be baptized.

This part of my life would not be complete without mention of something that occurred last year. My daughter, Mariah, asked me to give her a ride to the church so that she could audition for a play. Of course, I agreed, and we both went to the church. I was strictly functioning as a chauffeur only, or so I thought. But God was in charge. While Mariah was watching a video of the play, I was asked by the author of the play if I would consider playing a "small part" in this play. This is also something I NEVER envisioned. I agreed and for the next three months Mariah, Collin, and I practiced twice a week for the play, and I had an absolutely fabulous time.

At the time of this writing, I have been asked to pray about being a church elder. Now how miraculous is that. The drug addicted, convicted felon asked to be an elder in a community church. I prayed and God led me to agree to the training and I have been immersed in a study of how the early church began after our Lord's death on the cross. I am learning more each day as I study and believe that one of my God-given missions is to continue learning so that I might share with others the miraculous concept of grace and love that has been so freely given to me. It is in large part a central motivation for me to write this autobiography.

I had left St. Luke's Behavioral Health Center and went to work for an employee assistance firm that had purchased the EAP contracts from St. Luke's. This is where I was working on September 11th, 2001.

Every Tuesday morning Collin and I would go to the 7:00 am 12-Step meeting at the North Scottsdale Fellowship Club. On September 11th, 2001, we were on the way to Starbucks for coffee and hot chocolate before the meeting when the news came over the radio that the Twin Towers in New York City had been struck by an airplane. The initial report was that this was likely an accident.

I turned the truck around and went back home. Turning on the T.V., I saw for the first time the images of that first plane striking the first tower. In those first moments, the sadness and bewilderment were soon eclipsed by the tremendous, intense anger I felt when the fact that this was no accident began to emerge. Then when the news of the second plane striking the second tower came, I was overwhelmingly angry and afraid. The fear was in not knowing what would come next.

In the days that followed I remember waking Ellen up and talking to her about it and that I had an intuitive sense that I would be going to New York as a part of a crisis response team. Ellen didn't know why I had this intuition so she just accepted it as more musings from her husband. We had other issues to deal with anyway. First, we had these kids who were now seven and two years old. How were we going to deal with all the media hype and responses from people in their world? We first prayed and then mutually pledged that we would not bring the images of those attacks into our home. We decided that there would be plenty of opportunity for she and I to get as much information as we needed about the situation without unnecessarily exposing them to the horror of those images; we also decided that we would limit our discussions of the attacks while in our home so that the attacks and resulting fear would not be the focal point of our lives and subsequently the lives of the children. I like to think that we did a fairly good job of it.

I was working at an employee assistance firm at the time. This was a firm that provided external employee assistance services to client companies throughout the United States. Rick C., my clinical supervisor, and I had worked together at St. Luke's Behavioral Health Center in Phoenix. He was not only my supervisor, he was also a good friend. He, his wife, and their daughter had been to our home for dinner or parties on several occasions.

Once I arrived at work in downtown Phoenix, Rick and I discussed the situation. We knew that the call would likely come for volunteers to respond to the situation in New York City. Rick had hired me on at St. Luke's because of my law enforcement background as well as my experience with critical incident debriefings. So we both deduced that it would only be natural for the EAP firm to look for those with experience to respond to any needs from client companies in New York. When he asked me how I felt about going to New York, I told him that I would consider it an honor and privilege to serve in that way. Rick assured me that if the call came he would recommend that I be among those who were sent.

Meanwhile, the entire nation was in the process of responding to these cowardly and devastating attacks on the people of our country. It was no surprise to me that not one single client I had scheduled for that day kept their appointment. I remember sitting in that office talking on the phone to Ellen and other friends trying to make sense out of what happened. Even today it is tough to come up with words to fully express the sadness and compassion I felt for those killed in the attacks, or the anger that surfaced for those who killed innocent people for the sake of some political cause.

One of the takeaways from my experience is the Spirit of those who responded. Their selfless response to the calls to the towers is incalculable in terms of commitment, service, and dedication to ideals that very simply make this nation the best on earth. In the months and years that followed, I was privileged to observe a nation respond to the Spirit of those who gave everything in their attempt to rescue those trapped in the towers. I have been most richly blessed by having been witness to these courageous and meaningful actions of others.

Within a few days, the call came for me to go to New York City to do debriefings for the client companies we served in the vicinity of Ground Zero. In the first few moments after accepting the assignment, I felt proud, humble, and terrified. All my fear of flying issues began to emerge when I realized that I would be *flying* into the very city where airplanes had been used as weapons of mass destruction. The sheer lunacy of the moment was upon me and I had to deal with it!! Ellen was great at helping me; she and some girlfriends were on one of the first flights authorized after the No Fly Ban had been lifted. She and her friends had flown up to Las Vegas and back with no problems – more evidence that I had nothing to worry about.

One of the most significant events prior to my leaving was telling my kids where I was going and why I was going there. Kevin, at age 14, was first. He and I sat down and I told him that I would be going to New York to do debriefings with folks around Ground Zero. His response was pride that his father would be called into service for such a monumental cause.

Next, I told Collin, who was seven years old. His response was so emotional for me it made my eyes sweat! He told me that he was afraid and didn't want me to die. Now we had done a good job of limiting how much both Collin and Mariah had seen of the attacks, but kids and teachers he had contact with were processing the information at school so he had formulated an idea of what was going on. I am so glad that Ellen was there when we told him. We both did our best to comfort him and explain what my role would be and that I would be able to talk with him every day. That seemed to help him, and again Ellen was so good at helping this young boy work through this very real situation.

Mariah was next. Now at two years old she was very clued into people's emotions and responses to situations. So on some level she knew that daddy was going somewhere for something important and there was some element of potential concern for what he was doing. I will never forget holding that baby girl in my arms and talking with her about going to New York City. She looked at me after I had explained that I was going there and her little eyebrows furrowed as she appeared to be deep in thought. Suddenly, her face relaxed and she smiled at me as she asked "Are you going there to help people daddy?" When I told her that I was indeed going there to help others she said, in a way only Mariah can, "Okay daddy... you can go."

So I made the arrangements and found myself boarding an airplane exactly a week after two planes had been used to kill several thousand people. That plane was to leave from Phoenix, Sky Harbor, and land in Minneapolis, Minnesota. As I said earlier, I am not a big fan of flying and I noticed that each of my fellow passengers was resolute; there was very little talking or interaction between the passengers. Even the flight attendants, while trying to be cordial, friendly, and upbeat, were wearing that knowing look of trepidation that I felt, and that I am quite certain the others were also experiencing to some degree. I recall that I had recently purchased a book on The Prayer of Jabez, and I was content to quietly read this book during the uneventful flight to Minneapolis. I noted that there were several empty seats on the flight; in fact, the empty seats outnumbered the occupied ones. Once the plane landed and those leaving had deplaned, I noticed how quiet we were, how lost in our own thoughts. I know I was trying to deal with the fear of flying and with the fear caused by a new set of thoughts that had come to mind. With all the devastation in New York, what was I going to bring to this mix? How in the world was I gonna be able to help anyone? How could I possibly know the depth of their pain? These thoughts were interrupted by the captain notifying the nine remaining passengers going from Minneapolis to New York that we were preparing for takeoff.

On this flight, I noticed that my heart skipped a beat, and I had trouble breathing when I observed a passenger get up from his seat and move forward to use the lavatory, thankfully. In that moment, I made eye contact with another passenger, a burly and swarthy looking man. When our eyes locked we realized that we had initially had the same thoughts. He spoke first, saying that he was glad that the other man had gone to the lavatory instead of to the cockpit. I finally exhaled, smiled, and told him me too! In that moment, it felt comforting to me that I was not the only one having all these thoughts. After that, we had a brief conversation mostly about how few folks were on the plane and how much we were aware of little things that previously we didn't pay much attention to.

The landing was pure terror for me. Likely a textbook landing for the pilot, but for me sheer terror! Anyone who has flown into LaGuardia Airport knows that it is nestled on an inlet and is nearly surrounded by water. Of course, never having flown there before, all I could see was water! My fearful mind invented all sorts of reasons for our descent--none of them good--and I couldn't understand why nobody else was upset about our plane plunging rapidly toward the water. I just knew that the pilot was gonna splash this plane. Looking back now, I am somewhat amused to let readers in on how inefficiently my mind works. Sometimes I compare my mind to a dark alley--I really don't want to be in there alone!! At any rate, land appeared, and the pilot put the plane down expertly and my New York adventure was soon to begin!

The company had made arrangements for me to stay at the Sofitel New York Hotel, in Manhattan. I took a very exciting cab ride from LaGuardia to the hotel. I would tell my wife and parents that I was previously unaware that a person would be able to operate a vehicle while engaging me in an eye-to-eye conversation while I was in the back seat and he was driving. How we did not crash, I have no idea. Soon I was deposited at the hotel and was able to check in and get to my room. Phone calls home came first. When I spoke with Ellen and the kids, it was magical. I missed them and wanted to be there; they were happy that I was safe and in a hotel. This was only one week after the attack on the Trade Center, and we as a country were not used to this kind of attack on our own soil, and we not sure that the terror was over. This was particularly evident when I spoke with my parents, particularly my father. I recounted the flight and cab ride and my dad asked where I was relative to the airport and Trade Center. I confessed that I didn't know but I had observed that everything in New York was built upward, almost the exact opposite of Arizona where everything is spread out. I assured him that any plane attack would be futile because I was in a hotel that was surrounded on each side by several buildings, so I believed I was safe.

Next I had to contact Alan P., who worked for the same company that I did. He had traveled to New York from his home in Washington State. We talked on the phone and agreed to meet for dinner at the hotel. I was surprised to learn that his daughter had accompanied him on the trip at her own expense. Alan was an easy-going man in his late 40s and his daughter was a delightful young woman in her mid-20s. I was fascinated to learn that in the aftermath of the attacks she had sought a way to assist those in need; when she learned that her father had been assigned to see people in New York, it was only natural for her to accompany him and volunteer her services in whatever way she could. We enjoyed a wonderful meal together, sharing our histories and passion for helping others; we parted to our respective hotel rooms knowing that in the morning we would meet for breakfast and then go over to the office and meet the counselors who lived and worked in New York.

When morning came we went to the office and found two female counselors whose lives had been overwhelmed with calls for counseling and crisis response in the aftermath of this horrific attack on the city and country. These two women had provided counseling services for client companies in and around the Trade Center for years. Their caseloads had increased exponentially once the attacks occurred and we were there to fill in the gaps in service that these kind souls were unable to meet due to the overwhelming demand. Tactically, we had to determine who was best suited for which jobs. Since I had experience with critical incident debriefings, it was quickly decided that I would be assigned to do those. I learned that there was a backlog of requests, so I began immediately lining them up. As it turned out, I would report to the business office each day, receive a list of companies that were requesting services, and then I would make my way to the various locations and debrief the people who were interested in receiving services. At times, I would also be on site at locations and would do some one-on-one work with individuals who were either in the buildings and were able to evacuate safely, or who had been near the buildings and had witnessed the destruction, devastation, and death, or who had been impacted in some different way by this situation. I will describe some of the situations that held particular meaning for me.

One that stands out for me is the woman who told me that she had worked in the towers for years and had chosen that day to stay home and process relationship issues with her boyfriend. She called in sick and both had gotten up and were seated in the living room of their high rise apartment. Their view from that living room afforded them unobstructed vision of the towers, and she described the absolute horror of watching both jets impact each tower. The incident so greatly impacted them that they both immediately left the state and went to stay with relatives in a neighboring state.

Another group's office was located within 10 blocks of the Trade Center. The office meeting room afforded those gathered clear view of the Trade Center. As a meeting was in progress in that room on that Tuesday morning, they were startled as a huge passenger jet flew directly past their building at their level and within seconds slammed into the first tower. People in that debriefing told me that they had been able to read numbers and writing on the plane as it flew past their office.

Still another woman told me of being in the tower and fleeing the building immediately after the impact. She described being so terrified that she began running until she reached relative safety and turned to see the fire in the building. Overcome with terror, sadness, and shock, she began walking and did not stop until her bloodied feet would not allow her to continue. She then sat down and cried for hours until others came to her aid.

Another woman described the following situation. Having worked in the towers for some time, she had taken to using the daycare center near the towers for her young child. As was her custom, she dropped her child off at the day care center and went to work. When the first plane hit the first tower, she immediately went to the day care center and retrieved her child and intuitively left the area on foot. Meanwhile, across town, her husband had learned of the attack and with no way of contacting his wife began a trek that took him into the area of the towers. After several hours of walking and fighting his way to as close as he could, he saw that the area around the Trade Center had been destroyed in the collapse of the towers. Believing that both his wife and child were dead, he buckled from sheer exhaustion and grief. He did not learn their fate until the next day.

Finally, I spoke to a man who was in the first tower when the attack occurred. He recalled leaving the building quickly. Once at street level, he encountered debris falling from above so he sought temporary cover underneath some sort of parapet near the building. As he waited there, he described seeing papers, computer parts, airplane pieces, furniture, and other stuff falling to the street from above. He also described smelling the jet fuel and hearing loud, intermittent thumping noises coming from above him. As he and others gathered at the bottom of this tower, they decided to brave crossing the street in an effort to get away. Once on the other side of the street, this man was able to see that the thumping noise was the sound of people who had jumped or fallen out of the building and were landing on the parapet above him.

I spent time with lots of people, listening to their experiences during this monumental incident. I learned so much about the human spirit and the art of listening and validating another person's experience in life and death. I felt so humbled by these brave people who survived this monstrous attack on human life. As I listened, I couldn't help but think that maybe, just maybe, I had to experience all that I did to be effective in helping these folks make sense out of a senseless situation. I also came to grips with the notion that the help doesn't come from me; the Grace comes from a Power Greater than me. This spirit, Holy Spirit if you will, allows me to every once in a while get out of the way and just listen to and understand the experiences of people as they go through their lives. I will address this process in another chapter.

When I returned to Phoenix, Rick, my supervisor, helped to debrief me. He helped me make some sense out of all that I had seen and done. We processed the feelings of being overwhelmed, and the learning that came from simply listening with empathy to people who had been through so much. I am so grateful for Rick's role as both supervisor and friend.

Chapter 24

DEATH OF MY PARENTS

*I*n February 2004, I was working for the Daisy Mountain Fire Department as an employee relations specialist. I had been hired there by Chief Tom H. in a contract position and I enjoyed a working relationship with the fire crews, their supervisors, and management. The plan was for me to work that first year under contract and then evaluate the prospect of being hired on to the department on a full-time basis.

I had maintained contact with a number of the folks I had worked with or trained in my years as a clinician. One of those people was Diane E., who at the time I met her was the director of member assistance for the State Bar of Arizona. Diane was seeking certification as an employee assistance specialist and contracted with me to be supervised in the requisite number of hours to attain certification. We would often meet at the State Bar offices in central Phoenix. I was instantly drawn to the work she did with lawyers in the state of Arizona. I remarked to her one day that I would be interested in her job if she ever left. Diane was gracious enough to refer clients to me for counseling needs, and she also had me provide training to those attorneys who were in need of stress management or other coping strategies. Diane eventually left the State Bar to pursue her doctorate in psychology, and for nearly two years the Member Assistance Program functioned without a director.

In February 2004, a representative from the State Bar of Arizona called me to schedule an interview for the director's position. I was ecstatic until we got down to scheduling the interview. It seems that the only day they had set aside to interview candidates I had already booked something and was unable to move that booking. We anguished on the phone trying to arrange and rearrange time for this interview of a lifetime for me, but, with overwhelming sadness, I had to hang up the phone without being able to schedule the interview. Fortunately, the phone rang again and the representative informed me that the search committee really wanted to interview me and offered the option of doing the interview by telephone. I readily accepted and within the week participated in the telephone interview. Now truth be told, I am uncomfortable on the phone. I do much better face to face, so it was with a great deal of trepidation that I approached the interview. I recall that several people participated in the interview and it seemed to go well. At the end of the interview, someone asked if there was anything else I wanted the committee to know before they made their decision. I told them that I appreciated their time and willingness to extend me the opportunity of interview for the position and that I had the perfect face for a phone interview! Judging from the peals of laughter from the participants they appreciated my sense of humor. More importantly, they called back after a short deliberation and offered me the job!

It was through this work that I was introduced to The Commission of Lawyer Assistance Program or COLAP. This commission is a group of dedicated professionals who serve lawyers in the 50 states. Their primary focus has been to assist lawyers dealing with alcoholism or substance abuse issues. The time I spent at the State Bar of Arizona was one of the most rewarding periods in my life.

In June 2004, I took a group of kids to Ensenada, Mexico, as part of a church mission trip. Pastor Rod Layman and his wife Karen facilitated this trip and I was a driver and interpreter for Oasis Community Church. It was my first trip, and I was excited to be of assistance and to be part of an outreach to bring the Word of the Gospel to people who wanted to better know the Power and Saving Grace of Jesus Christ.

Prior to leaving, my mom had been admitted to the hospital for some complications associated with her heart condition. She had a year earlier also been diagnosed with lung cancer and had participated in both chemotherapy and radiation treatments. I spoke with her before I left and she told me that she would be fine and that I should go. I arranged for some time off from work and off to Mexico I went.

I had been there two days when another contingent from our church arrived. One of the pastors told me that I needed to call my wife immediately. Or course, I was alarmed but had no clue as to what Ellen was going to tell me. I made the call from a pay station in the city and learned that my mom's condition had worsened and, in fact, she had lapsed into a coma not long after I had left. Waves of guilt and fear flooded through me. Ellen said, "honey I think she's waiting for you to get back so she can go."

I left immediately. And God Bless those kids who I had driven there in the van; they unanimously elected to return early from this trip. We drove all through the night and arrived in Phoenix early on the morning of June 11, 2004. After dropping the kids off at their houses, I drove straight to Scottsdale Memorial Hospital. I found my dad, both my sisters, my niece, and her kids all gathered around my mom in the hospital room. When I got there, everyone greeted me and I greeted them. Within seconds, mom, after having been in a coma for several days, sat up, opened her eyes, smiled at everyone, and then laid back down, and within half an hour she crossed over. . Initially, I experienced feelings of guilt, sadness, and loneliness. I could write for days and not be able to sufficiently express how much I loved that lady.

In the days that followed, the intensity of my feelings permeated my every waking hour. I could not get away from the raw emotion that the experience of her passing brought to my life. Ellen was so gracious in allowing me my feelings. It also helped that several of my friends were able to share their common experiences with me in helping me to negotiate this difficult time in my life.

During this difficult time, I attended a 12-Step meeting daily for nearly a month. I am so thankful that I had that opportunity because living life on life's terms without resorting to the use of alcohol, drugs, or other self-destructive behaviors is not always easy. I can honestly say that throughout that time I did not want to drink, nor did I want to use cocaine. I simply didn't want to feel the way I was feeling. At each 12-step meeting I attended, I found a group of people whose primary purpose was to stay sober and help others to achieve/maintain sobriety, and that's exactly what and whom I needed.

Honestly, the death of my mother was more difficult for me to negotiate than the shooting and trial and being incarcerated, even more difficult to deal with than having my very life threatened. I kept telling myself that I could get through this loss; after all, I had been helping others deal with losses in their lives. I have learned that it's different when it directly impacts me. I am eternally grateful to my family, friends, and others who supported me through that time in my life.

On April 13, 2006, my father, Howard Nevitt, died in his sleep from liver cancer. Thankfully, through my mother's passing nearly two years earlier, I was prepared for the emotional onslaught. I experienced fear, guilt, and loneliness again, but the intensity and duration was not as acute as when mom left. I attended 12-Step meetings daily and learned that the feelings were intense but in a different way. I am very grateful for the contributions to my life made by these wonderful, hard-working, loving people.

Chapter 25

THEN THE STORMS CAME

*I*n 2005, Hurricane Katrina became the costliest natural disaster, as well as one of the five deadliest hurricanes, in the history of the United States. At least 1,836 people died in the actual hurricane and in the subsequent floods, making it the deadliest U.S. hurricane since the 1928 Okeechobee hurricane. Katrina caused nearly triple the damage wrought by Hurricane Andrew in 1992.

Katrina crossed southern Florida as a moderate Category 1 hurricane, causing deaths and flooding there before strengthening rapidly in the Gulf of Mexico. The storm weakened before making its second landfall in southeast Louisiana as a Category 3 storm on the morning of Monday, August 29.. It caused severe destruction along the Gulf coast from central Florida to Texas, much of it due to the storm surge. The most significant number of deaths occurred in New Orleans, Louisiana, which flooded as the levee system catastrophically failed, in many cases, hours after the storm had moved inland.

Within a week of the storm, I got called by an agency that I am affiliated with and was given the assignment of responding to Lafayette, Louisiana, to work with a government agency whose personnel were impacted by Hurricane Katrina itself. Their homes were destroyed and their families were injured, killed, or uprooted. I was teamed with a clinical psychologist from Colorado named Joe, who had arrived prior to me. The two of us were housed in a trailer on a government compound and we interacted with this group on a daily basis. Working in this fashion was effective from the standpoint of immersing ourselves in the day-to-day routine of these dedicated professionals who had themselves been traumatized by this natural disaster. Some of the most effective assistance we were able to provide came as a result of simply being in the vicinity of these folks as they were in process of doing their jobs despite having just had their own lives turned upside down by this hurricane. While our approach was less formal than the structure of critical incident debriefings I had participated in previously, the methodology proved effective. As the time passed, we became a part of their world and soon more and more of the individuals began to request time away from the group to process individual responses. In this manner, we were able to effectively serve this group in making some sense out of their individual and collective responses to the situation.

As the days progressed, I had developed a routine of rising early each morning and doing an hour of exercising and running. I would also call home and speak with Ellen and the kids. Then I would spend the day with the group. I had also made contact with Bill Leary, the director of the Louisiana Lawyer Assistance Program, a man whom I had met the year before. He was able to put me in touch with a lawyer in Lafayette who drove out to my location and took me to a couple of 12-Step meetings. I am so grateful for the social support network afforded by the American Bar Association's Commission on Lawyer Assistance Programs (COLAP), and the program of Alcoholics Anonymous. These two groups allow for people to be supported in their physical and emotional health across the nation, in Canada, and in England. So even in the midst of a natural disaster as monumental as Hurricane Katrina, this alcoholic was able to find a 12-Step meeting and thus receive instantaneous support from alcoholics and drug addicts who I had not previously met. The axiom of there being no strangers, only friends we haven't yet met, was the overriding principle in this situation. I am thankful to my friends Bill and Kathleen, two true friends, and the wonderful group of alcoholics and addicts in Lafayette, Louisiana, that helped this alcoholic stay sober during that time.

So a funny thing happened while assisting folks in making sense out of their reactions to Hurricane Katrina...Hurricane Rita showed up. Hurricane Rita was the fourth-most intense Atlantic hurricane ever recorded and the most intense tropical cyclone ever observed in the Gulf of Mexico. Rita caused $11.3 billion in damage on the U.S. Gulf Coast in September 2005. Rita was the third Category 5 hurricane of the historic 2005 Atlantic hurricane season.

Rita made landfall on September 23 between Sabine Pass, Texas, and Johnson's Bayou, Louisiana, as a Category 3 hurricane. The storm surge caused extensive damage along the Louisiana and extreme southeastern Texas coasts and destroyed some coastal communities. The storm killed seven people directly; many others died in evacuations and from indirect effects.

The storm system that became Rita formed at the tail of an old frontal boundary 95 miles east-northeast of Grand Turk Island; the system was moving west-northwest, towards Florida. Less than a day after forming, the depression became the 17th tropical storm of the season on September 18 and was named Rita. A mandatory evacuation was ordered for the entire Florida Keys.

As Rita entered the Gulf, rapid intensification began. National Hurricane Center advisories issued every three hours showed strengthening from 5 p.m. EDT on September 20 to 11 a.m. EDT on September 21, when Rita's maximum sustained winds increased to 140 mph. Rita continued to gain strength unabated. An update at 2:15 p.m. CDT said maximum winds had increased to 150 mph. Less than two hours later, at 3:55 p.m. CDT, another update reported that Rita had strengthened to a Category 5 hurricane, with maximum wind speeds of 165 mph. At 10 p.m. CDT, Rita reached its maximum intensity, with sustained winds of 180 mph.

In addition, residents of Cameron Parish, Calcasieu Parish, Acadia Parish, Iberia Parish, Beauregard Parish, Vermillion Parish and parts of Jefferson Davis Parish were told to evacuate ahead of the storm. Cameron Parish was hit the hardest with the towns of Creole, Cameron, Grand Chenier, Johnson's Bayou, and Holly Beach being totally demolished. Records around the Hackberry area show that wind gusts reached over 180 mph.

I had been working with the personnel at the governmental compound for several days. Each day, I would show up to the place I had dubbed "The War Room." This was a large conference type room that had maps of the weather regions of the Gulf of Mexico and surrounding states spread out on tables throughout this large room. Groups of people would be working with these paper maps, tracking the beginnings of a tropical storm that had begun to form in the gulf. Inescapable to the eyes, was a video screen of the entire Gulf of Mexico complete with water and land mass depictions and a developing storm colored mostly white on the water portion of the video screen. From the time I initially observed this storm, it grew every time I took my eyes off the screen and then returned my gaze to it. I kept eyeing where this storm was located and the distance between that location and Lafayette, Louisiana. That distance seemed to grow smaller with every passing hour. I started to get nervous. Now I had been calling home every day and in my conversations with Ellen, I assured her that everything would be fine. But every time I looked at that video screen I saw that the mass of the storm was growing, and the colors were not only white, but now the colors orange, red, and purple were appearing. I knew this held some meaning and it likely wasn't good. I asked one of the guys what the colors meant. It was explained to me that as such storms grow the wind gusts are depicted by color with white being the slowest and orange/red being the highest. So my suspicions were confirmed, this was a big, fast moving, growing storm and it was moving through the Gulf of Mexico toward us.

My poker face must have slipped because now the guys realized that I was nervous. The taunts began. "What's the matter Hal, you scared?" The truth was "yes, I am scared," so I decided to go with that. That admission just brought more good natured teasing, with people asking if they could have my clothes, other belongings, etc. We all laughed, but I really was wondering how I was going to make it out of this situation. Within an hour, the call came to evacuate the area. Now here was a dilemma: We were being told to evacuate to higher ground, but we didn't have a place to go, or a vehicle with which to get there.

I talked with my newfound recovering friends--some were leaving, but most were staying. Joe and I conferred and decided that we were going to stay. We also decided that we would need to gather food, water, and other supplies and make alternate arrangements for shelter because all we had was a sleeping trailer. First, we went into town for supplies. We found a local retail store and the scene in the parking lot was something I have not seen before or since. People were very close to panic; the look in people's eyes spoke of unmitigated fear. I saw people fighting over cases of water and food. We got in, got what we needed, and got out of there as quickly as we could. I was praying the entire time: "God, grant me the serenity to accept the things I cannot change, courage to change the things I can, and Wisdom to know the difference."

Once we made it back to the compound I located the building maintenance man, an older guy who I had spoken with while out exercising early each day; his name was Ray-Beau. He had a southern drawl and a slow deliberate way of speaking that just brought calmness and serenity to any situation. That was exactly what I needed. I told Ray-Beau that I wanted him to pretend that the storm was right outside the compound; I pointed to the parking lot and asked him to imagine that storm/hurricane being right there. Once he told me he had that image in his mind, I told him that I wanted to know where he would go in that compound if that hurricane was in the parking lot. Ray-Beau's face brightened and a big smile came to his face as he said, "Mr. Hal, you come with me; Ol' Ray-Beau gonna show you what you want." I followed him into the building and he took me to a place he called the "mud room." "Mr. Hal, this the zact spot you wanna be when that ol' hurricane come." The room was rather large; it had only one entrance and there was a large floor drain that ran almost moat-like around the entire room. There was a thick glass window on one side but otherwise thick walls made it as secure as could be. I had found my spot to hunker down when the storm came. I thanked Ray-Beau, and, bless his Cajun heart, he put his hand on my shoulder and told me that it was all gonna be good—"nothin' bad gonna happen here!"

Once back outside to gather my belongings and our supplies I noticed that the sky had literally turned into one big cloud that was slowly turning. It was spectacular to behold, yet foreboding at the same time. My phone rang. It was Ellen. "How are you? Oh, I'm ok, how are you?" She tells me that she's been watching the news and from the videos she's been watching it looks to her like Hurricane Rita is going to make landfall very close to Lafayette, Louisiana. "No way honey...it's gonna hit way away from here." Something in my voice must have betrayed me because she told me that she knew I was exaggerating some (not her exact words)! So then and there I told her what was going on. I told her that Ray-Beau had found us a great spot and all would be well. I told her specifically that God had not brought us this far to drop me on my butt. We exchanged "I love yous" and she told me that she would never forgive me if I got killed in this deal, and I acknowledged that. For me this was a particularly tender moment because of the real-life nature of what was happening to each of us. I really do love that woman, and I am so grateful that she loves me!

We hunkered down for the night. The winds and the rains came. I prayed to God that he would protect us and others in the path of this great storm. He did. I actually was able to get some sleep. During a moment of particularly strong wind and rain, Joe and I decided to open a door to the outside to take a picture. Big mistake! First, as I attempted to open the door I was nearly sucked outside into a veritable wall of water buffeted about by wind. The next thing I noticed was the wind dying down some and the rain pelting down onto the water pooled on the ground. When the wind came back, the same raindrops that had been dropping down began to be shot, and I mean like rifle shots, through the open door. I took a few in the head and chest and I can say that they were traveling with such force as to actually hurt as they struck my body. With Joe holding my arm so I wouldn't be whisked away, we got the door shut, not to be opened again until the wind and rain stopped. Years later, I would read about a football player being sucked up and dropped by hurricane/tornado winds; I'm so happy that didn't happen to me. Thank you God!!!

Sometime in the early morning hours the storming stopped. As my eyes opened and I realized I was alive, I thanked God and marveled at how much raw power that hurricane had. Outside, the land bore the evidence of a powerful, unforgiving storm. Trees, power lines, house parts, and other debris dotted the landscape around the compound; as people emerged from homes, hand waves were exchanged as well as shouts of praise that we were alive. I am so very grateful for that experience, particularly the fact that I survived. A call home to Ellen and the kids was next. We exchanged shouts of joy and praise to God for bringing us through this alive. Next, I was ordered to get myself home as quickly as possible.

That was going to prove problematic. Flights in and out of Lafayette were canceled and would not resume for an indefinite period of time. My only option was to get to Baton Rouge. My best friend Nik had called from Arizona and had actually offered to drive out, pick me up, and bring me home. And I believe he would have done it. But as it turned out, my good friend Ray-Beau was not there to assist me. As we were talking about my dilemma, he told me that one of his daughters was going to Baton Rouge the next day and would be glad to drop me off at the airport! Way to go Ray-Beau! So I was driven to Baton Rouge the next day, got on a flight home, and made it back to family, friends, and Phoenix in one piece.

Etched upon my mind is the calm and peace of the street I live on. As I pulled into the driveway, I paused for a minute and thanked God for getting me home safely. As I walked up the driveway, I could hear the laughter of my family through the open front door. Conan and Bella, my two boxers, were waiting, wagging, and talking to me as I got to the front door. It was great to be home!

Chapter 26

THE POWER OF CHOICE

I have recounted these instances in an effort to help those reading this to understand that the recovery process is so much more than simply stopping drinking or using drugs. I needed to mend fences with people, and there are other aspects of recovery that are equally important.

The process of recovery from addiction, that is recovery from a hopeless condition of mind, body, and spirit, has given me great comfort in knowing that I never have to return to those dysfunctional behaviors ever again. There is a saying among a group of my peers: "While the monkey is off my back...the circus is still in town." I have taken this to mean that recovery is a day at a time proposal. For me, each day when my eyes throw open I am dealing once again with untreated alcoholism and drug addiction. That being said, it is imperative that I enact a number of behaviors to deal effectively with that condition. Prayer, meditation, and other activities that serve to maintain my spiritual condition are necessary for me.

First and foremost, I believe wholeheartedly that in life every one of us will be tested. There will come a time when we all must live out our certain truths. Thus came the realization for me that life often gives us the test, then teaches the lesson. So how does a police officer, educated, trained, and raised in a culture where loyalty, discipline, and ethical behavior are highly valued, deviate so far from that path? This is a question that I have struggled with in some form or another for the past twenty some odd years. The answer to this question is sometimes simple, yet there are times when the reasoning gets clouded, And at times, I'm frustrated and angry with myself for choosing and behaving so poorly.

So there is no misunderstanding, let me say from the outset that I am 100% accountable for every choice I made. I have not always thought this way, but for me to affect any sort of recovery from drug addiction, and the accompanying behaviors, I had to arrive at the place where I could, without equivocation, say "I made that choice and got this result from that choice." To most people, this sounds so simple, and, in reality, it is simple, but it was not easy for me to get to this place. The combination of socialization, biology, and my own misguided perceptions and thought processes created the opportunity for me to choose poorly and reap the consequences of those choices.

It is this power of choice, which each of us has, that allows us to determine the path we will take, even when our actions produce results we did not anticipate, like, or want. That's where the test comes because now the combination of my thinking and behaving has created some form of challenge for me, not to mention for others. Discouragement, disillusionment, fear, and other feelings will come, but with determination, humility, and perseverance we are capable of making choices that bring better results.

The descent into this pit of despair and darkness was agonizing. I knew intuitively that I could not last in this place. I so much wanted to turn myself in; I wanted the insanity to stop, but fear kept me from doing this. I knew that there would be no forgiveness for allowing myself to become addicted and for behaving criminally. The conflict that raged inside of me was an intense interaction between intellect and emotion. I knew in my heart that what I was doing was wrong and yet my brain was always ready to rationalize, minimize, or justify my behavior and the impact that it was having on others. I would learn later that these very dynamics are present in the majority of people who are addicted to substances or processes.

My street identity allowed me to act out by looking like a dirtbag, hanging around bars with other addicts. I was always drinking alcohol, living outside the bounds of moral, ethical, or lawful behavior. It became easy to use all sorts of mind games to convince myself that my behavior was normal. Some of my favorites were: "Everyone else is doing this" or "I'm not really addicted; I need to use this to think better." My absolute favorite was "If you had my life, you would drink/use drugs this way too." What absolute bullshit. It's so easy to see that now, but at the time I truly was able to convince myself that I was justified in doing what I did.

Eventually, I was able to pierce the thick wall of denial I had used to cocoon myself in. Without question I was not able to do this on my own. I needed/need input from others. I had several change agents in my life who were willing to help with this task. I initially blamed a long list of people for my problems. These included the prosecutor, the judge, the police department, politicians, my lawyers, people in my treatment group, people at 12-Step meetings, family, and others. I had so many fingers pointed out at everybody else. The problem with this strategy is that the focus is on changing everyone but me, and, in reality, the one who needed to change the most was in fact me!

Ultimately, through the combined process of treatment, support group attendance, working through those 12 steps, and imprisonment I was forced to confront myself. I remember being locked up in a cell for behaving badly while in the prison; there's a clue. While confined in disciplinary segregation, I literally came face to face with me. What an awful, yet change laden moment! In that cell, there was no glass mirror, only a stainless steel plate, and the only image looking back was mine. I had finally run out of other people to blame for my condition. It was in that moment that I caught the vestiges, the rudiments, of personal accountability. Slowly, haltingly, ever so painfully, I came to a place where I recognized that my behavior put several people in tough places. To achieve any peace it became necessary for me to acknowledge that I had put certain people in those tough spots, this kind of thinking was a radical departure from the victim mentality of "How they had wronged me."

Oh how it stung to have to admit that through my own selfishness I had brought this all on myself. Painful as it was, it was necessary for me to acknowledge my part. I have no idea why I didn't go through with the plan to end my life in despair, nor do I have any idea of why I have managed to stay sober all these years. I do know the how of it; the how is contained in the process of applying the principles of the 12 Steps to my life.

From that meager beginning, I have learned that the recovery process is affected on a daily basis. I have definitely come to believe that what I have is a daily reprieve from the ravages of addiction, contingent upon the maintenance (and expansion) of my spiritual condition. Simply put, I could not stop the addiction process by attending 12-Step meetings; that was a start, but without the process of working through the 12 steps of the recovery there would be little in the way of lasting change in me. It is only fitting at this point that I express how grateful I am to the process of sponsorship. Having a program sponsor is an essential piece of my recovery process. Seeing the 12 Steps etched into the life of another man is absolutely necessary for me. My current sponsor, Michel S., has been a veritable life line for me as I have negotiated some monumental occurrences in my personal and professional life; without his help, I am sure that I would be closer to drinking and using again.

I recognize the arguments of many others who have sobered up, cleaned up, and gone on to live lives of distinction without practicing the 12 steps of recovery. I can only speak for myself, and my experience. Even today, after several years of not consuming alcohol or drugs, I begin each day with untreated alcohol and drug addiction. For me, and perhaps only me, I need to do certain things to ameliorate the effects of those addictions. I find those things in practicing the 12 steps. Thank you God for bringing me to and through these experiences!

Chapter 27

REDEMPTION, COURAGE, AND THE POWER OF GOD

*R*edemption means receiving forgiveness or <u>absolution</u> for past mistakes, and protection from disgrace. This story would not be complete if I did not speak specifically of this concept. Moreover, I am convinced that my life experience has been nothing short of miraculous. I became hopelessly addicted to drugs, was incarcerated in a prison, and literally damned to a life of despondent, miserable ineptitude. After all that, I was redeemed to a life of freedom from the bondage of self; I received a new and lasting joy, freedom from the fear of people and economic insecurity, and, most of all, the opportunity to recognize that no matter how far down the scale I traveled, my experience may benefit others.

I don't know about anyone else, but I am of the opinion that God knew. He knew that I would make choices that would lead to a time of trial, discord, self-doubt, injury, despair, and darkness. He knew that I would need others in my life to help create the vision of redemption in my mind, heart, and soul, and He knew that I would need His Grace and Strength to take the steps to complete the picture. That first step of faith was to see myself in a different role, one in which I was thinking differently, feeling differently, and, ultimately, behaving differently.

I began to visualize myself succeeding. That was not easy to do while I was locked up in prison. But even there I had opportunities to practice. Helping to create and form that softball team was such an opportunity. I witnessed first-hand how my enthusiasm was infectious and the impact it had on others. I realized in that process how important it is to nurture my dreams; to identify those things that are honorable, good, fair, and right; and to focus my thoughts on those things and work at bringing those things to bear on situations in my life.

That enthusiasm was an outward manifestation of the spirit and passion that a kind and loving God placed within my heart, soul, and mind.. The God of forgiveness and, most of all, the God of redemption. The enthusiasm and hope given me by my Creator has created a positive energy that is, to this very day, palpable to those in my life. And I must be honest and say that more often than not my enthusiasm, or the God within me, carries me beyond any skill or talent that I might have. Although I make many, many mistakes in my daily life, I have a deep and abiding respect for people, and I know that everyone is struggling with something today. It is often my vision or ability to see the potential in others that is helpful to those struggling to see their own potential.

For me to extract the most from the experience, it was necessary for me to have the courage to endure the painful feelings associated with the event. It has been through this endurance that I have been taught and guided by my experiences. My expression of commitment to this ideal comes in the form of doing my absolute best to live my life one day at a time, and truly one moment at a time. I have come to believe that I wasted a great deal of my life by letting the essence of my life slip through my fingers by living in the past or attempting to live in the future. It actually takes a great deal of courage to live in each moment as it unravels before us. For me, courage is equated to confidence. I don't believe that we are born with confidence; we have to develop it. It comes from having tried and failed, repeatedly. It came to me by actually confronting my fears and then living to tell the story of my experience. Courage is a very personal issue as well, and I firmly believe we are all capable of developing physical, moral, and spiritual courage. In fact, I believe that we all have the capability to demonstrate courage;we just need a circumstance for its expression.

Courage is that quality of mind and spirit that allows us to face danger, pain, or difficulty. It does not mean the absence of fear. Those without fear are reckless, irresponsible, and thoughtless. Those without fear often bring harm to themselves or others. Courage is manifest when we encounter risks; by taking risks, and either succeeding or failing, we learn how to be brave. Courage acknowledges the fear and carries on in spite of it; courageous people tell themselves: "I refuse to let this circumstance, or the fear of this circumstance stop me from doing my best." Remember that fear may accompany any attempt at greatness; accept the fear, relish it, acknowledge the need for a power greater than self, and then do it.

No life, marriage, business, dream, or project can succeed without perseverance. This can be the most elusive of all spiritual attributes. Those who don't achieve their goals don't fall short from a lack of ability; they simply gave up too soon. Conversely, those who are high achievers will tell you that sustained, focused activity, not "luck" or a "golden opportunity," led to their goal achievement.

Seemingly unbearable emotional pain can drive you to the brink of giving up on yourself, and your dreams. I have felt afraid and demoralized and have been one breath away from giving up. In these moments, I remember what one of my greatest teachers, Black Wally, would tell me every day: "Son, don't you quit ten seconds before the miracle happens."

As I read over the last section, it dawned on me that I would be remiss if I didn't include some ideas about imperfection. I struggle with the idea of making mistakes now that I have lived through some of the awful choices I made. I tell myself not to be afraid to admit that I am less than perfect. I continue to make mistakes on a daily basis--just ask my kids! I have come to believe that our collective imperfection is the fragile thread that binds us to each other; I fully believe that one thing that every human being has in common with every other human being is the fact that we are fearfully and wonderfully made, yet have the defect of making all manner of mistakes in what we perceive, think, and do!

I believe that it is in that falling short that my dependence upon God and His Grace becomes evident; and I am most grateful for a kind and loving God who is willing to treat me with the patience, tolerance, and kindness that I wish I could always extend to others.

When I accept my imperfection, and the imperfection of the world I live in, I am also in touch with the enduring Hope of Grace. I can fully grasp the concept of every day being a precious gift, and I can thus develop a passion for discovery and a commitment to making this a better place for myself and those who are around me. It is while in acceptance of my humanity that I am able to believe fully in the concepts of forgiveness and redemption.

In a previous chapter, I described the vicious nature of addiction as a dark, soul sucking, merciless, incapacitating cloud that colors every aspect of a person's life. Certainly this is an accurate description of what addiction meant in my life.

For me, the biological, psychological, social, and spiritual sickness that is addiction is not fully addressed, or effectively arrested, without the presence of Grace. Now, before you think that I am on a crusade to spiritualize or convert the entire world to some form of religiosity, bear with me a moment in my attempt to clarify my personal experience. All the while I was becoming physically and psychologically dependent upon drugs and alcohol, I was, on a conscious level, totally unaware of what was happening. Perhaps the most cunning, baffling, and powerful aspect of my addiction was in *thinking* that I knew what was happening to me, and around me, when, in reality, I had no idea of reality.

The key for my recovery is in recognizing that the phenomenon of attachment/addiction was accomplished through an unconscious learning process, and this learning occurred on an embedded physical level that eventually ruled my every living moment. It became as natural as breathing in and breathing out. To arrive at this knowledge was simply miraculous and was indeed an act of Grace, a Grace given me by my creator. It did not happen all at once; there was no burning bush or "white light" experience for me. Rather it took a combination of events and circumstances occurring in my life to bring me to a state of awareness as to the true nature of addiction, and the strategies necessary to affect recovery from the pernicious grip of this attachment.

As I write this today, I am convinced by my experience--I do not pretend to know the experiences of anyone else--that my recovery from the hopeless conditions of body, mind, and spirit would not have been possible without the Grace afforded to me by a kind and loving God. Before I go on, let me clarify that it is my belief that everyone who is attempting to recover from such a condition has experienced significant spiritual growth, perhaps disguised as pain/problems; and it is likely that each experience is as unique as the person experiencing such growth. Thus, when I talk of my experiences and beliefs I am not saying that any other human being's experience has to be either similar to mine, or limited by my narrow range of thought/intuition.

Even in the concept of choice God gives us Grace. Grace is there in either an effective or ineffective choice. It is in the giving of the choice that Grace appears in my life. I have heard it said that on a daily basis my choice is to live life on life's terms, and to ultimately grow spiritually through the experience, or to die a slow torturous death of being addicted to substances and processes that drain my life away. Sometimes I allow my brain to think that I don't like either of these choices. Thankfully, I have managed to turn those thoughts around through my association with people who support my continued spiritual growth.

It is my belief that Grace is the active expression of God's love for me. I have listened to sermons on Grace and heard pastors say that Grace is "unmerited favor from God." In writing about this, I'm unsure today if that is accurate, although I can point to several instances in my life when that definition could apply. For instance, surviving prison as a former police officer was obviously something that could not be accomplished without the Grace of God; staying sober through that ordeal, through my divorce, through the deaths of family members, and through the false allegations of my behavior was possible only through the Grace of God. All of these examples are rightly categorized as instances of Grace in my life. Here is where the uncertainty arises for me; my current concept of God is such that he continually "graces" me on a daily basis, and I'm not sure why, or what would now be "unmerited." God's love is so very constant that even when I make mistakes his loving kindness is obvious and overwhelming.

The Grace afforded me has allowed me to become who I am today. I have the ability to go where other free men go, provided that I am on sound spiritual footing. I have actually gone back into the very prison where I was incarcerated, and into the very room where I processed so many of the steps to freedom with my 12-Step sponsor. And in that very room I gave to a prisoner my contact information and he did contact me and in fact attended my church for a time upon his release. There are other instances where I have been able to do what my Creator has asked me to do only through Grace. Indeed, there are times when I have been relieved of the bondage of self and given the privilege of working with others to address the evil that is addiction.

I know that I have been in the desert/arena called life. I was there either by my choices, or the choice of my Creator. It has been in those deserts that I have learned to trust and to have faith that my God is there for me and Graces me daily with His presence. In a very real sense, I have returned home to be that which my Creator intended me to be. On some days, I am an awesome husband; on some days, I am an awesome father; and on some days, I am an awesome friend, boss, co-worker, etc. All this is due to the Grace of God as it appears in my life. And then there are days that I fail miserably at the ideals that either I set for myself or that others expect of me. It is in each of these realities that I can be comfortable in knowing that my God's Grace will carry me, that He will never leave me. When I look back over my life I can see the difference in the footprints along the path, and I know that it is His Grace that carried me when I was most desperately in need!

When I set out to write this book I spoke with several of my friends about my central message. That message is this: "Don't give up! Don't give up on yourself, or the power of your Creator!!" My sincere hope is that you can take the ideas and concepts that I have expressed and apply them to your situation in a way that brings hope to you and those whom you will meet on your journey.

Stay alive long enough to tell others of your experience. Know that you and your experience are valuable. That which you have lived through and the sharing of it with others have the potential to save lives!

The fact that you are reading this is an active affirmation of your desire to live and to develop meaning and purpose in your life. Take one more breath and break through the pain, confusion, and fear. Cling to the idea that life is worth living in spite of all that may seem out of place right now.

It takes courage to face the past and rise above what has already happened. It takes courage to acknowledge the difficulty that life presents, and faith to know that through a relationship with God and the support of friends, mentors, and spiritual guides, you can walk through the wreckage and get to the other side. And when you do, you can rest in the knowledge that you have found the will of your Creator and have followed that direction.

If you are still reading this then there is an overwhelming likelihood that you have, at some point in your life, given your time, talents, and resources to someone or something for the betterment of that person or cause. Just as certain is the concept that the desire and energy to do for others was given you by the Holy Spirit of God. I am challenging you to take that same energy and direct it back to yourself. Take care of yourself biologically (eat well, drink the right stuff, exercise, and get the rest you need), psychologically (read the right stuff, listen to the right stuff, and nurture your spirit), and socially (surround yourself with the right people, interact with others, play, and pray). The energy to nurture is there, and there for a reason; make sure to apply it to yourself.

I am often called upon to address groups on the topic of overcoming adversity. I often end my presentation by telling the audience that I'm not going to wish them luck, or tell them I hope they do well. I am telling you the same thing. Luck has no place here; any type of gain requires effort, not luck. Make the effort, whatever effort your situation calls for; remember that the universe rewards action. Make a plan and follow through.

Finally, know that you already have done well! There are so very many goals you have accomplished, and adverse situations that you have overcome. You don't need me or anyone else's hope that you do something awesome.

You already have. Now go do more!!!

AUTHOR BIO

Hal Nevitt, a licensed substance abuse counselor and social worker, continues his practice in the heart of Arizona. Hal graduated from Arizona State University and has over 16 years of experience.

9 781948 382519